P9-CFP-166

The Great Depression

OPPOSING
VIEWPOINTS®
DIGESTS

The Great Depression

DON NARDO

Greenhaven Press Inc., San Diego, California

Library of Congress Cataloging-in-Publication Data

Nardo, Don, 1947–
    The Great Depression / Don Nardo.
        p.   cm. — (Opposing viewpoints digests)
    Includes bibliographical references and index.
    Summary: Presents contrasting viewpoints about the best remedies for the economic crisis of the 1930's, the implementation of President Roosevelt's New Deal, and the historical impact of both the Depression and the New Deal.
    ISBN 1-56510-743-8 (alk. paper) — ISBN 1-56510-742-X (pbk. : alk. paper)
    1. New Deal, 1933–1939—Juvenile literature.
2. Depressions—1929—United States—Juvenile literature. 3. United States—Economic policy—1933–1945—Juvenile literature. 4. United States—History—1933–1945—Juvenile literature. 5. United States—History—1919–1933—Juvenile literature. [1. New Deal, 1933–1939. 2. Depressions—1929. 3. United States—Economic conditions—1918–1945.]   I. Title. II. Series.
E806.N27   1998
973.917—dc21   97-31173
                                                CIP
                                                AC

Library of Congress: Cover Photo, 9, 12, 19, 49, 54, 61, 77, 81, 94
National Archives: 88

CONTENTS

FOREWORD

"The only way in which a human being can make some approach to knowing the whole of a subject is by hearing what can be said about it by persons of every variety of opinion and studying all modes in which it can be looked at by every character of mind. No wise man ever acquired his wisdom in any mode but this."

—John Stuart Mill

Greenhaven Press's Opposing Viewpoints Digests in history are designed to aid in examining important historical issues in a way that develops critical thinking and evaluating skills. Each book presents thought-provoking argument and stimulating debate on a single topic. In analyzing issues through opposing views, students gain a social and historical context that cannot be discovered in textbooks. Excerpts from primary sources reveal the personal, political, and economic side of historical topics such as the American Revolution, the Great Depression, and the Bill of Rights. Students begin to understand that history is not a dry recounting of facts, but a record founded on ideas—ideas that become manifest through lively discussion and debate. Digests immerse students in contemporary discussions: Why did many colonists oppose a bill of rights? What was the original intent of the New Deal and on what grounds was it criticized? These arguments provide a foundation for students to assess today's debates on censorship, welfare, and other issues. For example, *The Great Depression: Opposing Viewpoints Digests* offers opposing arguments on controversial issues of the time as well as views and interpretations that interest modern historians. A major debate during Franklin D. Roosevelt's administration was whether the president's New Deal programs would lead to a permanent welfare state, creating a citizenry dependent on government money. *The Great Depression* covers this issue from both historical and modern perspectives, allowing students to critically evaluate arguments both in the context of their time and through the benefit of historical hindsight.

This emphasis on debate makes Digests a useful tool for writing reports, research papers, and persuasive essays. In addition to supplying students with a range of possible topics and supporting material, the Opposing Viewpoints Digests offer unique features through which young readers acquire and sharpen critical thinking and reading skills. To assure an appropriate and consistent reading level for young adults, all essays in each volume are written by a single author. Each essay heavily quotes readable primary sources that are fully cited to allow for further research and documentation. Thus, primary sources are introduced in a context to enhance comprehension.

In addition, each volume includes extensive research tools, including a section comprising excerpts from original documents pertaining to the issue under discussion. In *The Bill of Rights*, for example, readers can examine the English Magna Carta, the Virginia State Bill of Rights drawn up in 1776, and various opinions by U.S. Supreme Court justices in key civil rights cases, as well as an unabridged version of the U.S. Bill of Rights. These documents both complement the text and give students access to a wide variety of relevant sources in a single volume. Additionally, a "facts about" section allows students to peruse facts and statistics that pertain to the topic. These statistics are also fully cited, allowing students to question and analyze the credibility of the source. Two bibliographies, one for young adults and one listing the author's sources, are also included; both are annotated to guide student research. Finally, a comprehensive index allows students to scan and locate content efficiently.

Greenhaven's Opposing Viewpoints Digests, like Greenhaven's higher level and critically acclaimed Opposing Viewpoints Series, have been developed around the concept that an awareness and appreciation for the complexity of seemingly simple issues is particularly important in a democratic society. In a democracy, the common good is often, and very appropriately, decided by open debate of widely varying views. As one of democracy's greatest advocates, Thomas Jefferson, observed, "Difference of opinion leads to inquiry, and inquiry to truth." It is to this principle that Opposing Viewpoints Digests are dedicated.

At War with the Depression: Roosevelt and the New Deal

For the traders on the floor of the New York Stock Exchange, the morning of Monday, October 21, 1929, seemed little different than most other average days. Behind the scenes, some financial experts were quietly worried; for after unusually large gains in September, prices had begun to slide a bit and the market had alternately stalled and surged during the first three weeks of October. Although this suggested instability, most people on Wall Street seemed generally calm. The economy of the United States appeared healthy and humming, and few doubted that the unbridled prosperity of the 1920s was destined to continue well into the foreseeable future. Only a few days before, on October 17, Yale economics professor Irving Fisher had delivered the reassuring message that prices had reached "what looks like a permanently high plateau." And he was confident that within a few months that plateau would be "a good deal higher than it is today."[1]

Such rosy predictions seemed to reinforce the optimism expressed by national leaders. In his well-known "rugged individualism" speech (October 22, 1928), soon-to-be-president Herbert Hoover had stated that

> the greatness of America has grown out of a political and social system and a method of control of economic forces distinctly its own—our American system— which has carried this great experiment in human welfare further than ever before in all history. We are

nearer today to the ideal of the abolition of poverty and fear from the lives of men and women than ever before in any land.[2]

Echoing this same theme, in his last speech in office (December 4, 1928), Hoover's predecessor, Calvin Coolidge, had said that the country should "regard the present with satisfaction and anticipate the future with optimism."[3]

But as the day of October 21 wore on, the highly overinflated bubble of national optimism began to burst. That afternoon stocks suddenly slumped sharply in the heaviest trading on record; trading was so intense, in fact, that by the end of

Crowds gather at the New York Stock Exchange building. When the U.S. stock market crashed on October 29, 1929, its effects launched a worldwide economic depression.

the day, the ticker machine used to record transactions was running a hundred minutes behind the actual sales. In the days that followed, things only got worse. On the following Monday, the market registered an unprecedented loss of $14 billion. And on Tuesday, October 29, it took another enormous jolt, losing $15 billion and bringing the losses for the month to a staggering $50 billion.

The great stock market crash of October 1929 signaled the onslaught of a severe economic depression that affected not only the United States, but most of the rest of the industrialized world as well.[4] It became known as the Great Depression because it was the worst financial crisis ever recorded in modern times. For up to a decade or more, tens of millions of Americans and hundreds of millions of people worldwide fell into grinding, seemingly unrelenting poverty and suffered untold deprivations and miseries.

Business Caught in a Fatal Tailspin

What had caused this catastrophe that almost no one had anticipated? Part of the problem was that too many people had purchased more stocks than they had cash to pay for, opting to buy "on the margin," that is, on credit from their brokers. Then, frightened by initial dropping prices, speculators began rapidly to unload their stock portfolios, sending prices even lower, creating a crashing downward spiral. Historian Gerald W. Johnson explains how the effects of this disaster quickly rippled outward, engulfing the rest of society:

> When the panic of 1929 suddenly wiped out the whole value of many stocks and sharply reduced the values of others, a great number of people who had thought themselves rich, or at least well-off, found themselves with much less than they had thought they had, or with nothing at all. By [the] millions they quit buying anything except what they had to have to stay alive. This drop in spending threw the stores into trouble, and

they quit ordering [new products] and discharged clerks. When orders stopped the factories shut down, and factory workers had no jobs.[5]

Whatever the cause of the crisis, its effects were clearly devastating. Unemployment rates, which had wavered at about 3 percent before October 1929, rose to 9 percent by early in 1930. And in the next two years, this rise continued to a crippling 25 percent (this was the overall rate; as many as half of all black Americans were jobless). Between the time of the stock market crash and the end of Hoover's presidential term in 1933, over nine thousand U.S. banks failed and closed their doors. Some four thousand of these, with combined deposits of $3.6 billion, closed in the first two months of 1933 alone. Because depositors had no insurance to back up their money, millions of Americans lost their entire life savings in a fleeting, tragic instant.

With the stock market and banks disabled, many businesses went into a fatal tailspin. In 1930, 26,355 U.S. businesses failed, a debilitating figure that, to the nation's horror, was exceeded the following year when 28,285 more went under. The corporations that were still in business in 1932 had a combined deficit of $5.64 billion, a staggering figure at the time; and in that same year the nation's volume of manufacturing was only 54 percent of what it had been before the 1929 crash.

"Buddy, Can You Spare a Dime?"

These stark figures exemplify the great scope of the crisis; yet mere numbers cannot convey the toll of hardships and suffering endured by individuals and families across the land. Their stories are much more illustrative and powerful. After visiting North Dakota, a newspaper reporter wrote:

Last winter the temperature went down to 40 below zero and stayed there for ten days, while a 60-mile wind howled across the plains. And entering that kind

Children stand while eating their Christmas dinner in this Great Depression–era photograph.

of winter we have between 4,000 and 5,000 human beings . . . without clothing or bedding, getting just enough food to keep them from starving. No fuel. Living in houses that a prosperous farmer wouldn't put his cattle in. . . . They now have 850 families on relief, and applications are coming in at a rate of 15 or 20 a day.[6]

Describing a similar plight, a tenement dweller in East Harlem, New York, wrote to his congressman, "It is now seven months I am out of work. . . . I have four children who are in need of clothes and food. . . . My daughter who is eight is very ill and not recovering. My rent is [over]due two months and I am afraid of being put out [evicted]."[7] In another part of New York City, struggling songwriter Yip Harburg testified:

> I was walking along the street . . . and you'd see the
> bread lines . . . fellows with burlap on their shoes were
> lined up all along Columbus Circle, and went for
> blocks and blocks around the park, waiting. . . . The
> prevailing greeting at that time, on every block you
> passed, by some poor guy coming up, was: "Can you
> spare a dime?" Or: "Can you spare something for a cup
> of coffee?" . . . "Brother, Can You Spare a Dime?"
> finally hit on every block, on every street.[8]

Harburg turned that plaintive phrase into what became a sort
of Great Depression anthem with which nearly everyone
identified. Its sad refrains went in part:

> They used to tell me I was building a dream
> With peace and glory ahead
> Why should I be standing in line
> Just waiting for bread? . . .
> Say, don't you remember, they called me Al
> It was Al all the time
> Say, don't you remember I'm your Pal!
> Buddy, can you spare a dime?[9]

Few could spare even a dime to help American farmers,
who were among the hardest hit, especially in the first few
years of the crisis. Writer John Steinbeck captured their plight
in this moving excerpt from his classic novel *The Grapes of
Wrath*:

> And then the dispossessed were drawn west—from
> Kansas, Oklahoma, Texas, New Mexico; from Nevada
> and Arkansas families, tribes, dusted out, tractored out.
> Carloads, caravans, homeless and hungry; twenty
> thousand and fifty thousand and a hundred thousand
> and two hundred thousand. They streamed over the
> mountains, hungry and restless. . . . The kids are hun-
> gry. We got no place to live. Like ants scurrying for
> work, for food, and most of all for land. . . . And the

dispossessed, the migrants, flowed into California, two hundred and fifty thousand, and three hundred thousand. Behind them . . . [other] tenants were being forced off [their lands]. And new waves were on the way, new waves of the dispossessed and the homeless, hardened, intent, and dangerous.[10]

Other homeless or hopeless Americans found themselves no longer able to face the evictions, the bread lines, the forced migrations, or the faces of their hungry children; and so they took their own lives. "This depression has got me licked," went the suicide note of a Houston mechanic.

There is no work to be had. I can't accept charity and I am too proud to appeal to my kin or friends, and I am too honest to steal. So I see no other course. A land

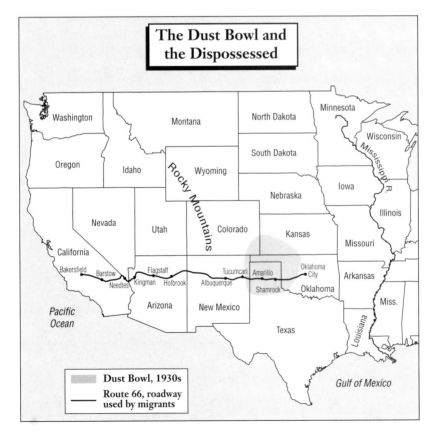

The Dust Bowl and the Dispossessed

Dust Bowl, 1930s
Route 66, roadway used by migrants

flowing with milk and honey and a first class mechanic can't make an honest living. I would rather take my chances with a just God than with unjust humanity.[11]

Hoover Endorses Self-Reliance

The federal government's response to this overwhelming national crisis was, on the whole, inadequate. In large degree this stemmed from the conservative attitude of the top leaders, beginning with President Hoover (served 1929–1933). They believed it would be unseemly and dangerous for the federal government to provide massive free aid, or "government charity," and that the best approach to alleviating the crisis was to rely on the strength of Americans to help themselves, aided by private charities and state and local relief efforts. Noted historian T.H. Watkins explains:

> This was . . . the very ethos of a white, Protestant culture, the image that Hoover and his kind held up as the ideal of Americanism. Hard work, honesty, and independence, they believed utterly, had brought this country to the forefront of nations, had built a breed of men (and women, too, some conceded, though not often) who had taken the institutions of the founding fathers and made them the wonder of the world. Anything that might weaken the strength of that tradition would weaken the very character of America and was, by definition, evil. Government charity, especially, by robbing people of initiative, would be the very embodiment of error. The national government should stay out of the personal lives of its citizens, even if they were in trouble.[12]

Expressing this philosophy in a February 1931 press statement, Hoover stated:

> This is not an issue as to whether people shall go hungry or cold in the United States. It is solely a question

of the best method by which hunger and cold shall be prevented. It is a question of whether the American people . . . will maintain the spirit of charity and mutual self-help . . . as distinguished . . . from appropriations out of the Federal Treasury for such purposes. . . . If we break down this sense of responsibility and individual generosity . . . in times of national difficulty and if we start appropriations of this character we have . . . impaired something infinitely valuable in the life of the American people. . . . Once this has happened . . . we are faced with the abyss of reliance in future upon government charity in one form or another. . . . I am confident that our people have the resources, the initiative, the courage, the stamina and the kindliness of spirit to meet this situation in the way they have met their problems over generations.[13]

Some powerful political and industrial leaders took the idea of personal initiative a step further by suggesting that the economic crisis was mainly the result of the laziness and poor work ethic of the masses. The Depression, contended automobile tycoon Henry Ford in March 1931, had developed because "the average man won't really do a day's work unless he is caught and cannot get out of it. There is plenty of work to do if people would do it."[14] A few weeks after delivering this elitist gem, Ford quietly laid off over 75,000 of his own workers.

Despite such attitudes, Hoover and his administration must be credited with an earnest, if highly limited, effort to halt the economic downslide. The most significant part of that effort was the creation early in 1932 of the Reconstruction Finance Corporation (RFC), whose mission was to loan money to failing banks, railroads, insurance companies, and other big businesses. The theory was that if these institutions became solvent, they would put people back to work and thereby stimulate the economy. As Hoover's secretary of the treasury, Ogden Mills, stated it, "I want to break the ice by lending to industry so that somebody will begin to spend in a big way."[15] The RFC did save many businesses and was also helpful when it began loaning money to individual states late in 1932. But it was the only major federal program created to combat a crisis of epic proportions, and by itself it was simply not enough.[16]

A Change of Direction for the Country

In contrast, the administration of Franklin D. Roosevelt that took office in March 1933 enacted many federal programs designed to combat the ravages of the Great Depression. Roosevelt was a fifth cousin of the twenty-sixth president, Theodore Roosevelt (1901–1909). The younger Roosevelt, who became known as FDR, had gained notoriety as assistant secretary of the navy during World War I and as a vice presidential candidate in the election of 1920.[17] Soon after losing that race, he suffered a more tragic loss—that of the use of his legs in a bout with polio; however, in an impressive display of courage and determination, he reentered politics, serving as governor of New York during Hoover's presidential term. Running against Hoover in the 1932 campaign, Roosevelt won by a landslide, garnering 472 electoral votes to the incumbent's 59.[18]

Roosevelt thought that the crisis could only be alleviated by the government's taking a fresh approach—that the country needed a "new deal" from its leaders; and his presidency and programs came to be described and defined by that catchphrase. He had not revealed the huge scope of his plans during the course of the campaign. But listening to his inaugural address, delivered on March 4, 1933, the American people began to realize that the country was about to undergo a major change of direction. Dropping the usual political and feel-good rhetoric of such speeches, Roosevelt leveled with the American people in the opening lines. "This is a day of national consecration," he said in sober, stirring tones, "and I am certain that my fellow-Americans expect . . . [that] I will address them with a candor . . . which the present situation of our nation impels. This is pre-eminently the time to speak the truth, the whole truth, frankly and boldly." It was time for a change of attitude, he said, for facing and conquering the nervous, gnawing fear of the unknown that presently gripped the country. "The only thing we have to fear is fear itself—nameless, unreasoning, unjustified terror which paralyzes needed efforts to convert retreat into advance." How could that conversion be accomplished? By "treating the task as we would treat the emergency of a war," he asserted.

> We must act, and act quickly. . . . If we are to go forward we must move as a trained and loyal army willing to sacrifice for the good of a common discipline, because, without such discipline, no progress is made, no leadership becomes effective. . . . I am prepared under my constitutional duty to recommend the measures that a stricken nation in the midst of a stricken world may require. . . . I shall . . . wage a war against the emergency as great as the power that would be given to me if we were in fact invaded by a foreign foe.[19]

The new president wasted no time in revealing the legislative weapons he planned to use in his war against the Depression; and it was plain that his measures would go far beyond those of the Hoover administration. The strategy of the New Deal was to attack the crisis forcefully on a number of fronts. In contrast to Hoover's conservative approach, in which government played a minimal role, Roosevelt called for direct and vigorous intervention by the federal government in revitalizing businesses, creating new jobs, providing food and other relief for the needy, and instituting dramatic systemwide reforms.

Implementing the New Deal

Roosevelt's opening salvo against the Depression came on March 6, just two days after he had assumed office. As part of a national "bank holiday," all banks had to close down and show their books to federal inspectors. Based on their assess-

President Franklin D. Roosevelt believed the devastating effects of the Great Depression could be alleviated by his New Deal—an innovative strategy that used federal intervention to revitalize business and provide relief to the needy.

ments, the government extended emergency aid to those banks that needed it; and only those whose finances were sound were allowed to reopen. With this one sweeping gesture, the president ended the national banking crisis and restored public confidence in the country's banks. About a week after declaring the bank holiday, he wrote to an old friend, "We seem to be off to a good start and I hope to get through some important legislation while the feeling of the country is so friendly."[20]

These words turned out to be an understatement of the first magnitude. The first three months of Roosevelt's first term, now commonly called the historic "Hundred Days," witnessed one of the most ambitious spurts of presidential-congressional activity in American history. "In the face of an unprecedented national economic crisis, Roosevelt managed to bend the legislature to his will. Congress became almost literally his rubber stamp as he submitted and saw passed into law one sweeping legislative bill after another. Never before or since did a U.S. president hold such commanding authority or enjoy the backing of so many diverse groups of Americans."[21]

The first two of Roosevelt's sweeping New Deal bills were the Agricultural Adjustment Act, submitted to Congress on March 16, and the Civilian Conservation Corps (CCC), presented on March 21. The Agricultural Adjustment Administration (AAA) was designed to increase the profits of poor farmers by having them reduce production of wheat, corn, rice, and other crops. The theory was that if these foodstuffs became a bit more scarce, they would be worth more, so their prices would increase a little, putting more money in farmers' pockets. The CCC's goal was to provide work for the many jobless young men between the ages of eighteen and twenty-five. Between 1933 and 1941, the CCC paid some 2.7 million Americans to plant trees, build dams, fight forest fires, and so on, giving them both skills and the means to support their families while helping to reduce the unemployment rate.

One of the New Deal's most far-reaching programs, one that affects nearly all American wage earners and retirees to this day, was the Social Security Act, signed into law on August 14, 1935. The purpose of Social Security was and remains to aid citizens who are in need because of increasing age, unemployment, or sickness. Contributions from both employers and wage earners go into a fund that distributes the money to people over the age of sixty-five, temporarily out of a job, or too ill to work. "We can never insure one hundred percent of the population against one hundred percent of the hazards . . . of life," commented Roosevelt at the signing ceremony, "but we have tried to frame a law which will give some measure of protection to the average citizen and to his family against the loss of a job and against poverty-ridden old age." The law was also a cornerstone in the growing system of New

Deal programs, he added, a system "intended to lessen the force of possible future depressions."[22]

Building, Revitalization, and Jobs

Another of Roosevelt's bold and far-reaching programs was the Tennessee Valley Authority (TVA), one of the most ambitious construction projects in world history. The goal was to build fifteen huge dams in the Tennessee River valley. The benefits would be threefold: to provide millions of Americans with cheap electricity; to help control damaging floods that periodically ravaged the area; and to create years of work for tens of thousands of people. One of the TVA's directors, David E. Lilienthal, later offered this somewhat poetic overview of its accomplishments:

> This is the story of a great change. . . . It is a tale of a wandering and inconstant river now become a chain of broad and lovely lakes which people enjoy, and on which they can depend in all seasons. . . . It is the story of how waters once wasted and destructive have been controlled and now work, night and day, creating electric energy to lighten the burden of human drudgery. Here is a tale of fields . . . [grown] vigorous with new fertility . . . of forests now protected and refreshed . . . of people and how they have worked to create a new valley.[23]

Building, revitalization, and jobs were also major themes of Roosevelt's Public Works Administration (PWA).[24] This federal agency contracted with private companies to construct school and college buildings, hospitals, roads, bridges, sewage systems, and other public works in all but three of the nation's 3,073 counties. By 1939 the PWA had employed about half a million workers per year and financed 34,508 projects at a total cost of about $6 billion. Many of these projects were worthwhile and useful thanks largely to the tireless efforts of the agency's scrupulously honest director, Harold L. Ickes, Roosevelt's secretary of the interior.

The New Deal Not a Panacea

Like the president, Ickes dreamed and planned on a grand scale and wanted to do far more—for instance, to clear all the nations' slums, to build superhighways from ocean to ocean, and to erect affordable housing for everyone who needed it. There existed at the highest levels of government the feeling that the New Deal might not only end the Depression, but also create a new, infinitely better country. In October 1934 Ickes recorded in his diary that Roosevelt

> has great imagination and I told him the other day when I was lunching with him that if he had been president at the time when the Treasury was over-flowing, he would have gone down in history as the greatest builder since the world began. He probably will anyhow if we go ahead with such a program as we are discussing.[25]

But despite many sweeping and constructive achievements, Roosevelt, Ickes, and other leading New Dealers often tend-ed to dream bigger than they could deliver. Roosevelt did not become the "greatest builder," for although the CCC, TVA, PWA, and a number of other programs enjoyed varying degrees of success, some New Deal efforts were failures. One notable example was the Civil Works Administration (CWA):

> Begun in October 1933, the program was designed to put as many Americans to work as possible in the short-est amount of time. At first, it seemed to be on the right track. By January 1934, the CWA had more than 4.2 million people on its employment rolls; but the problem with the program was that it was too unstructured. A lot of people were receiving federal money for questionable or trivial endeavors—raking leaves, for example—and Roosevelt himself saw that the potential existed for cre-ating a class of "reliefers" who might become perpetual-ly dependent on the government.[26]

Accordingly, Roosevelt admitted his mistake—a rare move for a politician—and closed down the CWA in April 1934.

The New Deal was not, therefore, the ultimate panacea for the nation's economic woes that Roosevelt would have liked it to be. In spite of some real gains, the country's financial recovery was slow and unsteady. It was also at times highly selective. Some groups, particularly minorities, most notably black Americans, had *two* obstacles to their getting ahead—economic bad times and ingrained prejudice; and not surprisingly, governmental programs that helped many white people gave nonwhites only very limited relief.

In addition, some Americans continued to believe, along with Hoover and most Republican leaders, that Roosevelt's "big government" approach to recovery was immoral, wrongheaded, and dangerous. "The people know now the aims of this New Deal philosophy of government," Hoover stated during the 1936 election campaign (in support of Republican candidate Alf Landon).

> We [the Republican opposition] propose instead leadership and authority in government within the moral and economic framework of the American system. . . . We propose to demobilize and decentralize all this spending upon which vast personal power is being built. . . . The New Dealers say that all this that we propose is a worn-out system; that this machine age requires new measures for which we must sacrifice some part of the freedom of men. Men have lost their way with a confused idea that governments should run machines.[27]

The World War

Those Republican proposals were not enacted. Roosevelt and the Democrats won the 1936 election (and the 1940 and 1944 elections as well) and the New Deal remained firmly in place. Exactly how much it contributed to the eventual national recovery is difficult to say. In the early 1940s, the country entered World War II and the economy became supercharged by the enormous avalanche of U.S. war production, which turned out to be the largest single factor in the Allied defeat of Germany, Italy, and Japan. As scholar John C. Chalberg remarks, "In the final analysis, the American defense industry proved to be the ultimate public works project."[28]

Thus, the philosophy and overall effectiveness of the New Deal remains controversial. New Deal critics contend that Roosevelt conducted a large, expensive, and ineffective experiment that continually failed to balance the federal budget, greatly increased the national debt, and built a huge, unwieldy bureaucracy. Roosevelt's defenders counter that the New Deal helped nearly to double national income in its first seven years, employed millions of jobless, desperate people, and, most importantly, restored the country's morale, which had reached an all-time low during the Depression's early years.

Continuing Debate over Unanswered Questions

Greenhaven's *The Great Depression: Opposing Viewpoints Digests* examines the key facets of this debate about the effectiveness of the New Deal in alleviating the economic crisis of the 1930s. The essays in chapters 1 and 2 consist of opposing arguments over the impending implementation of New Deal programs and are accordingly presented in the context of their time. By contrast, chapter 3 presents the arguments of later scholars and statesmen, either praising or criticizing Roosevelt's New Deal achievements in the uncompromising light of historical perspective. Overall, the concise, opinionated essays in this volume convey the fact that, despite intense scrutiny of the Great Depression and New Deal in thousands of books and articles over seven decades, many questions about these important aspects of America's past are still, and indeed may always be, unanswered. Did the New Deal really make a dent in the Depression? How did the crisis and Roosevelt's answer to it affect the later development of the country? "Such questions," historian Morton Keller points out, "will not soon have their definitive answers. But they will be asked again and again as succeeding generations seek to explain, in terms satisfactory to themselves, the historical phenomenon of the New Deal."[29]

1. Quoted in T.H. Watkins, *The Great Depression: America in the 1930s*. Boston: Little, Brown and Company, 1993, p. 40.

2. Quoted in Richard Hofstadter, ed., *Great Issues in American History: A Documentary Record, Volume II, 1864–1957*. New York: Vintage Books, 1960, p. 343.

3. Quoted in Samuel Eliot Morison, *The Oxford History of the American People*. New York: Oxford University Press, 1965, p. 939.

4. European countries depended a great deal on American credit, and when that credit became nearly worthless, trade between Europe and North America suffered. In this and other ways, the economies of the United States and most European nations, as well as the other countries with which Europe traded, were so closely linked that the economic upheaval in America inevitably affected everyone.

5. Gerald W. Johnson, *Franklin D. Roosevelt: Portrait of a Great Man*. New York: William Morrow, 1967, pp. 119–20.

6. Quoted in Watkins, *The Great Depression*, p. 125.

7. Quoted in Howard Zinn, *A People's History of the United States*. New York: HarperCollins, 1980, p. 379. The threat of eviction was very real. In 1932 alone, approximately 230,000 American families were forced from their homes for nonpayment of rent.

8. Quoted in Studs Terkel, *Hard Times: An Oral History of the Great Depression*. New York: Random House, 1970, p. 20.

9. "Brother, Can You Spare a Dime?" (1932). Words by E.Y. Harburg, music by Jay Gorney. Quoted in Diane Ravitch, ed., *The American Reader: Words That Moved a Nation*. New York: HarperCollins, 1990, p. 270.

10. John Steinbeck, *The Grapes of Wrath*. New York: Viking Press, 1939, pp. 317–18.

11. Quoted in Anthony J. Badger, *The New Deal: The Depression Years, 1933–1940*. New York: Farrar, Straus and Giroux, 1989, p. 11. The national suicide rate rose from 14 per 100,000 in 1929 to 17.4 per 100,000 in 1932. The rate was much higher in many cities; in Minneapolis, for instance, it peaked at 26.1 per 100,000 in 1932.

12. Watkins, *The Great Depression*, p. 61.

13. Quoted in William S. Myers and Walter H. Newton, *The Hoover Administration: A Documented Narrative*. New York: Charles Scribner's Sons, 1936, pp. 63-64.

14. Quoted in Zinn, *A People's History of the United States*, p. 378.

15. Quoted in Badger, *The New Deal*, p. 48.

16. The RFC survived the transition to Roosevelt's administration, and when combined with other strong federal programs, it became a powerful tool in the national recovery. Under the direction of Roosevelt's appointee, Texas banker Jesse Jones, the RFC used many of its funds to buy banks' stocks, rather than simply to lend them money. This approach expanded their credit and capital rather than their debt and thereby gave banks more financial stability.

17. Roosevelt ran with James W. Cox on the Democratic ticket, which lost the election to the Republican team of Warren G. Harding and Calvin Coolidge.

18. The popular vote was 22.8 million to 15.7 million. The Democrats also captured both houses of Congress, winning the House by 310 to 117 and the Senate by 60 to 35.

19. Franklin D. Roosevelt, "First Inaugural Address," in Hofstadter, *Great Issues in American History*, pp. 352–57.

20. Franklin D. Roosevelt, "Letter of March 13, 1933, to John S. Lawrence," in Elliot Roosevelt, ed., *FDR: His Personal Letters, 1928–1945*, (Vol. 1.). New York: Duell, Sloan and Pearce, 1950, pp. 338–39.

21. Don Nardo, *Franklin D. Roosevelt: U.S. President*. New York: Chelsea House, 1996, pp. 59–60.

22. Franklin D. Roosevelt, "Presidential Statement upon Signing the Social Security Act, August 14, 1935," in Samuel I. Rosenman, ed., *The Public Papers and Addresses of Franklin D. Roosevelt*, Vol. 4. New York: Russell and Russell, 1969, p. 324.

23. Quoted in Richard Hofstadter et al., *The United States: The History of a Republic*. Englewood Cliffs, NJ: Prentice-Hall, 1957, p. 666. By the beginning of World War II, the TVA was producing two billion kilowatt-hours of electricity for eighty-three munic-ipally owned utility companies in Tennessee and neighboring states. Eventually the pro-ject generated over twelve billion kilowatt-hours, not only providing affordable power for homes and businesses, but also making possible the country's massive production of aluminum for ships, vehicles, and weapons in the war.

24. Although they were separate programs, $50 million in PWA funds helped to finance the TVA's dam-building efforts.

25. Harold L. Ickes, *The Secret Diary of Harold L. Ickes: The First Thousand Days, 1933–1936*. New York: Simon and Schuster, 1954, p. 206.

26. Nardo, *Franklin D. Roosevelt*, p. 74.

27. Herbert Hoover, "Challenge to Liberty Speech of October 30, 1936," in Hofstadter, *Great Issues in American History*, pp. 359–60.

28. John C. Chalberg, "Introduction," in William Dudley, ed., *The Great Depression: Opposing Viewpoints*. San Diego: Greenhaven Press, 1994, p. 21.

29. Morton Keller, "Introduction," in Morton Keller, ed., *The New Deal: What Was It?* New York: Holt, Rinehart and Winston, 1963, p. 5.

CHAPTER 1

Suggested Remedies for the Economic Crisis

"The New Deal will help America by substituting broad-based and resolute action for the Republicans' inaction; it will begin to reverse the downward economic spiral that has been perpetuated and hastened by that inaction."

The New Deal Will Help America

Author's Note: The essays in this chapter present opposing arguments over the impending implementation of New Deal programs and are therefore stated in the first person and the context of their time, namely, the early 1930s.

The nation needs a new, markedly different approach to managing its economy and ensuring prosperity for all Americans. Stating the need for a national change of direction, presidential candidate Franklin Roosevelt has given a memorable name to that fresh approach:

> I pledge you, I pledge myself, to a new deal for the American people. Let us all here assembled constitute ourselves prophets of a new order of competence and courage. This is more than a political campaign; it is a call to arms. Give me your help, not to win votes alone, but to win in this crusade to restore America to its own people.[1]

The reason why his campaign is a call to arms, why the nation must be restored, and why we need Roosevelt's New Deal is simple. The Republicans, led by Harding, Coolidge, and

Hoover, have, over their twelve years in power, failed to ensure prosperity.[2] It was during their watch that the stock market crashed in October–November 1929, plunging the United States and most of the rest of the world into this horrendous mess called the Great Depression. And in his four years in office, President Hoover, clinging to the "old deal" policies of the conservative politicians of the past, has done little or nothing to reverse the downward economic spiral.

The reason for the Republicans' failure is plain: The philosophy behind their traditional old-deal approach is a myth and a sham. The signature catchphrase of that philosophy, "rugged individualism," is perhaps best defined as the belief that the federal government should, whenever possible, stay out of people's lives; more specifically, it should not intrude in the affairs of corporations and businesses; and financial

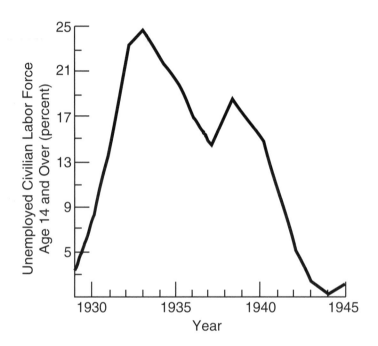

Unemployment, 1929–1945

The persistence of unemployment in the 1930s and its sharp rise in 1937 caused some economists to call for greater government spending to stimulate the economy.

Source: Historical Statistics of the United States, Colonial Times to 1970.

markets should be allowed to develop with very minimal, if any, federal regulation. But in reality, this is only a smoke screen designed to hide the true goal of this conservative philosophy—to allow those with money to keep on making more. "Closely examined, what is this creed of individualism?" asks noted historian Charles A. Beard. "Let the government maintain peace, defend property . . . and observe economy in expenditure—that is all," he answers. But do the so-called rugged individualists actually believe in this creed? Not at all, says Beard. This is because the creed, stripped of all flashy rhetoric, means getting money, simply that and nothing more. And to this creed may be laid most of the shame that has cursed our cities and most of the scandals that have smirched our federal government. . . . The cold truth is that the individualist creed of everybody for himself and the devil take the hindmost is principally responsible for the distress in which Western civilization finds itself. . . . Whatever merits the creed may have had in days of primitive agriculture and industry, it is not applicable in an age of technology, science, and rationalized economy. Once useful, it has become a danger to society.[3]

Thus, the old-deal individualist creed is not about self-determination and righteous rejection of "government charity," but rather about making money. The proof is that its chief proponents are not above accepting such charity when they need it. Indeed, those who cry the loudest that big government is bad are often the first to ask, even to demand, that government bail them out. As Roosevelt has so eloquently put it during the campaign:

While it has been American doctrine that the government must not go into business in competition with private enterprises, still it has been traditional, particularly in Republican administrations, for business urgently to ask the government to put at private disposal all kinds of government assistance. The same man who tells you that he does not want to see the government interfere in business . . . is the first to go to Washington and ask the government for a prohibitory tariff on his product. When things get just bad enough . . . he will go with equal speed to the . . . government and ask for a loan. And the Reconstruction Finance Corporation [Hoover's agency created to loan money to big businesses] is the outcome of it.[4]

According to the rules of the old deal, then, it is acceptable for a rich businessman to ask the government to prop him up; but the average individual who does the same is a lazy bum looking for a free handout from public funds.

The evidence that the doctrine of rugged individualism is corrupt and its policies inadequate to deal with the present crisis can readily be seen in every city in the country. *Fortune* magazine recently reported that in New York City nearly a third of the workers are unemployed. Of these, "410,000 [are] estimated to be in dire want. . . . 150,000 families [are] receiving emergency aid while . . . 32,000 families [are] waiting to receive aid." In Chicago, 3,177 teachers "lost $2,367,000 in bank failures . . . and 759 . . . lost their homes." And in St. Louis, "one-eighth of the population . . . [faces] eviction and starvation."[5]

Hooverville

Even more appalling is the situation journalist Charles Walker discovered at the town dump at Youngstown, Ohio. "The place is . . . a shanty town," he writes,

> or rather a collection of shanty hamlets. . . . From 150 to 200 men live in the shanties. The place is called by its inhabitants—Hooverville. . . . The inhabitants were not, as one might expect, outcasts or "untouchables," or even hoboes. . . . They were men without jobs. Life [for them] is sustained by begging, eating at the city soup kitchens, or earning a quarter by polishing an automobile. . . . This pitiable village would be of little significance if it existed only in Youngstown, but nearly every town in the United States has its shanty town for the unemployed, and the same instinct has named them all "Hooverville."[6]

Clearly, so many people across the land need help that ordinary relief efforts are inadequate. Only the federal government possesses the large-scale monetary and organizational resources needed to combat the crisis in any kind of an effective way. "The state can do what no individual or private group can do," states the respected economist Stuart Chase.

> As Czar of the nation's money, it can expand or shrink the supply, rising above the limitations of the individual who must live within the rules. Governments make the rules. If the state desires to check deflation it can check it; to create employment on useful and worthy projects, it can create it; to augment purchasing power, it can augment it; Nobody else can do it.[7]

Candidate Roosevelt agrees. "While the primary responsibility for relief rests with localities," he says, "the federal government has always had and still has a continuing responsibility for the broader public welfare. It will soon fulfill that responsibility."[8]

Roosevelt here refers, of course, to his promised New Deal agenda for the nation. The New Deal will help America by substituting broad-based and resolute action for the Republicans' inaction; it will begin to reverse the downward economic spiral that has been perpetuated and hastened by that inaction. "As I see it," Roosevelt declares,

> the task of government . . . is to assist the development of an economic declaration of rights, an economic constitutional order. . . . Every man has a right to life, and this means that he has also a right to make a comfortable living. . . . Our government . . . owes to every one an avenue to possess himself of a portion of that plenty [that the country has the potential to produce] sufficient for his needs through his own work.[9]

Roosevelt asks, "What do the people of America want more than anything else?" His answer will surely prove to be *the* answer for our ailing nation: "To my mind, they want two things: work . . . and with work, a reasonable measure of security. . . . These are the values that this program [the New Deal] is intended to gain; these are the values we have failed to achieve by the leadership we now have."[10]

1. Franklin D. Roosevelt, "Speech of July 2, 1932, to Democratic National Convention," quoted in Samuel I. Rosenman, ed., *The Public Papers and Addresses of Franklin D. Roosevelt*, Vol. 1. New York: Russell and Russell, 1969, p. 659.

2. Warren G. Harding became president in 1921; he unexpectedly died in office on August 2, 1923, and the vice president, Calvin Coolidge, succeeded him the next day. Coolidge won the 1924 election and served until 1929, when Herbert C. Hoover, who won the 1928 election, succeeded him. Hoover then served until March 1933, when Democrat Franklin D. Roosevelt became the nation's thirty-second president.

3. Charles A. Beard, "The Myth of Rugged American Individualism," in Howard Zinn, ed., *New Deal Thought*. Indianapolis: Bobbs-Merrill Company, 1966, pp. 8–10.

4. Franklin D. Roosevelt, "Commonwealth Club Speech of September 23, 1932," in Richard Hofstadter, ed., *Great Issues in American History: A Documentary Record, Volume II, 1864–1957*. New York: Vintage Books, 1960, p. 346.

5. "No One Has Starved," *Fortune* (1932), quoted in William E. Leuchtenburg, ed., *The New Deal: A Documentary History*. New York: Harper and Row, 1968, pp. 7–8.

6. Charles R. Walker, "Relief and Revolution," *The Forum* (1932), quoted in Leuchtenburg, *The New Deal*, pp. 10–11.

7. Stuart Chase, *A New Deal*. New York: Macmillan, 1932, p. 143.

8. Franklin D. Roosevelt, "Speech of July 2, 1932," quoted in Rosenman, *Public Papers and Addresses*, Vol. 1, p. 658.

9. Franklin D. Roosevelt, "Commonwealth Club Speech," in Hofstadter, *Great Issues in American History*, pp. 349–50.

10. Franklin D. Roosevelt, "Speech of July 2, 1932," quoted in Rosenman, *Public Papers and Addresses*, Vol. 1, p. 657.

"There is . . . no way by which the objectives of a planned economy can be made to depend upon popular decision. . . . The planners must control the people. They must be despots who tolerate no effective challenge to their authority."

The New Deal Will Harm America

Make no mistake about it. The so-called New Deal that Franklin Roosevelt wants to foist on the American people will be not only ineffective, but in the long run, dangerous and harmful to our cherished ideals of liberty, self-determination, and honest work for honest pay. President Hoover has stated the problem this way:

> We are told by the opposition [the Democrats] that we must have a change, that we must have a new deal. It is not the change that comes from normal development of national life to which I object, but the proposal to alter the whole foundations of our national life which have been built through generations of testing and struggle, and of the principles upon which we have built the nation. . . . Our opponents are appealing to the people in their fears and distress. They are proposing changes and so-called new deals which would destroy the very foundations of our American system.[1]

Perhaps before they so casually throw our American system out the window, Mr. Roosevelt and the other Democratic leaders need to be reminded of what constitutes that system and why it has proven to be the best and most productive one in world history. Again, Mr. Hoover is our guide. In his justly renowned "rugged individualism" speech, given in October 1928, he explained the "social system which is peculiarly our own," saying:

> It is founded upon a particular conception of self-government in which decentralized local responsibility is the very base. Further than this, it is founded upon the conception that only through ordered liberty, freedom and equal opportunity to the individual will his initiative and enterprise spur on the march of progress. And in our insistence upon equality of opportunity has our system advanced beyond all the world.[2]

Thus, the system works so well because the central government plays a very minimal role, leaving the initiative for work,

Herbert Hoover

hiring and firing, invention, manufacturing, and marketing to individual people and businesses. This is what it means to be an independent and self-governing people.

By contrast, as Mr. Hoover points out, "When the federal government undertakes to go into commercial business it must at once set up the organization and administration of that business, and it immediately finds itself in a labyrinth [maze], every alley of which leads to the destruction of self-government."[3] What he means is that a big government that tries artificially to create and control business will only rob individuals of the right to do so in a natural way, on their own;

and in the process it will build up a dangerously powerful and entrenched bureaucracy.

Such a buildup of federal governmental power is dangerous because it will inevitably threaten our liberties. "The departure from our American system," declares Mr. Hoover, "which our opponents propose will jeopardize the very liberty and freedom of our people."[4] To be more specific, the threat posed to freedom by a big-government system like the New Deal is that such a system is founded on coercion. Mr. Roosevelt appears to prefer the idea of compulsory organization of the American people by a central government that will plan and indeed dictate what they can and cannot do. He admits openly that his system will be structured like the kind imposed during a war emergency, when the government, for the sake of national security, assumes more power than it dares to do in peacetime. The distinguished journalist Walter Lippmann here explains why this approach is so ominous:

> The waging of war must be authoritarian and collectivist [characterized by central control of production and distribution]. The question . . . [is] whether a system which is essential to the conduct of war can be adapted to the civilian ideal of peace and plenty. . . . I can see how and why the general staff can decide how soldiers should live under martial discipline; but I cannot see how any group of officials can decide how a civilian population shall live nobly and abundantly. . . . There is, in short, no way by which the objectives of a planned economy can be made to depend upon popular decision. They must be imposed by an oligarchy [small group of rulers] of some sort. . . . Not only is it impossible for the people to control the plan, but . . . the planners must control the people. They must be despots who tolerate no effective challenge to their authority.[5]

Another respected journalist, J. Frederick Essary of the *Baltimore Sun*, has similar worries, saying that Roosevelt might turn the office of president into "a virtual dictatorship." Perhaps it would "be looked upon both as a benevolent and a necessary dictatorship," given the severity of the economic crisis that grips us; but "soften the phrasing as much as one may," a New Deal presidency could well become a "temporary executive absolutism."[6] Indeed, the even more frightening potential exists that such a dictatorship might not be so temporary. "Benevolent despots might . . . be found," Mr. Lippmann suggests. "On the other hand, they might not be," for the people "cannot select their despots. The despots must select themselves, and, no matter whether they are good or bad, they will continue in office so long as they can suppress rebellion and escape assassination."[7]

The Alternative to the New Deal

What, then, is the alternative to this dangerous New Deal agenda that looms on the nation's horizon? How can we end this economic slump and restore prosperity while maintaining our liberty and integrity? Andrew Mellon, who has served as secretary of the treasury under Presidents Harding, Coolidge, and Hoover, suggests we do nothing.[8] In time, he predicts, the slump will bottom out and the economy will rebound all on its own; and in fact, if we allow nature to take its course, we will, in the long run, find ourselves with a much better country. "Let the slump liquidate itself," he says.

> Liquidate labor, liquidate stocks, liquidate the farmers, liquidate real estate. . . . It will purge the rottenness out of the system. High costs of living and high living will come down. People will work harder, live a more moral life. Values will be adjusted, and enterprising people will pick up from less competent people.[9]

Will the economic crisis end of its own accord as Mr. Mellon suggests? Noted economist Ray Vance thinks that it will. "This period of depression is drawing to a close from natural causes," he states, "and will probably show improvement [in the very near future] without any legislative controls."[10] If need be, Vance adds, to hasten the recovery, the government can cancel its international debts, lower its trade barriers, readjust the national budget, and inflate the currency. None of these measures would entail the government growing larger and intruding on private businesses and individuals.

Mr. Mellon and Mr. Vance talk about what government can and should do to relieve the crisis. As for what individual Americans can do, Mr. Hoover wisely points out that mutual cooperation within our communities would have a large positive impact:

> Cooperation to perfect the social organization, cooperation for the care of those in distress . . . cooperative action in the advancement of many phases of economic life. . . . It is in the further development of this cooperation and a sense of its responsibility that we should find solution for many of our complex problems, and not by the extension of government into our economic and social life. The greatest function of government is to build up that cooperation, and its most resolute action should be to deny the extension of bureaucracy.[11]

Such cooperation, coupled with individual determination and personal freedom, has been the key to American greatness so far. We need to reemphasize these traditional values, not fly, out of unreasoned fear, down the radical and dangerous path being blazed by Mr. Roosevelt and his New Deal.

---

1. Herbert Hoover, "Speech of October 31, 1932, at Madison Square Garden," quoted in William S. Myers and Walter H. Newton, *The Hoover Administration: A Documented Narrative.* New York: Charles Scribner's Sons, 1936, p. 516.

2. Herbert Hoover, "Rugged Individualism Speech of October 22, 1928," in Richard Hofstadter, ed., *Great Issues in American History: A Documentary Record, Volume II, 1864–1957.* New York: Vintage Books, 1960, pp. 338–39.

3. Hoover, "Rugged Individualism Speech," in Hofstadter, *Great Issues in American History*, pp. 340–41.

4. Hoover, "Rugged Individualism Speech," in Hofstadter, *Great Issues in American History*, p. 343.

5. Walter Lippmann, "Planning for Peace in an Economy of Abundance," in *The Good Society*. Boston: Little, Brown, 1937, pp. 91, 103–104.

6. J. Frederick Essary, "The New Deal for Nearly Four Months," *Literary Digest* (1933), quoted in William E. Leuchtenburg, *The New Deal: A Documentary History*. New York: Harper and Row, 1968, p. 25.

7. Lippmann, *The Good Society*, p. 105.

8. Mellon (1855–1937) was a wealthy financier and industrialist who made his fortune in banking, coal, oil, and aluminum. As secretary of the treasury, he pursued a policy of cutting taxes in an effort to spur business expansion.

9. Quoted in Herbert Hoover, *The Memoirs of Herbert Hoover: 1929–1941, The Great Depression*. New York: Macmillan, 1952, p. 30.

10. Ray Vance, "The Problem of the Business Cycle," *The Nation* (1932), quoted in William Dudley, ed., *The Great Depression: Opposing Viewpoints*. San Diego: Greenhaven Press, 1994, p. 75.

11. Hoover, "Speech of October 31, 1932," quoted in Myers and Newton, *The Hoover Administration*, pp. 517–18.

"It didn't matter to me whether there was a Depression or not. Bemoaning your fate gets you nowhere. I knew wherever you make an effort, you make headway."

Self-Help Will Alleviate Unemployment

The high levels of unemployment caused by the Great Depression are truly deplorable. People need to work, both for their own support and well-being and for the well-being of the country. However, a continuous stream of government handouts is not the way to stimulate employment and revive the economy. Long-term government charity—constituting a massive public welfare system—would be socialistic, dangerous, and destructive because it would, over time, destroy personal initiative, self-worth, and integrity. As noted banker Frank A. Vanderlip puts it in a statement quoted often (but not often enough it seems) of late: "Our present efforts in the direction of relief [that is, an increasing volume of free government handouts] have broken down self-reliance and industry. I profoundly believe that society does not owe every man a living."[1]

Indeed, the American people are perfectly capable of helping themselves and occasionally, when need dictates, of helping their neighbors to get through hard times. This is the approach that has always worked in the past and that made America great. President Hoover summed it up this way:

My own conviction is strongly that if we break down this sense of responsibility of individual generosity to individual and mutual self-help in the country in times of national difficulty . . . we have . . . impaired something infinitely valuable in the life of the American people. . . . The basis of successful relief in national distress is to mobilize and organize the infinite number of agencies of self-help in the community. That has been the way of relieving distress among our own people. . . . I recall that in all the organizations with which I have been connected over these many years [of public service] the foundation has been to summon the maximum of self-help. . . . I am confident that our people have the resources, the initiative, the courage, the stamina, and kindliness of spirit to meet this situation in the way they have met their problems over generations.[2]

Thus, the way to put people back to work is to help them to help themselves. This is the approach advocated by the eminent and successful industrialist Henry Ford, whom nearly all Americans admire for putting into practice the traditional American work ethic. Mr. Ford has been criticized by a few left-wing radicals for criticizing the idea of charity; but they have not had the decency to quote him accurately. "I do not believe in *routine* charity" are his exact words. "I think it a shameful thing that any man should have to stoop to take it, or give it." What he refers to here is long-term charity that makes people dependent on free handouts and gives them no means of escaping their predicaments. Instead, he advocates, charity should consist of giving those in distress the skills and tools with which to put themselves back on their own feet. According to Mr. Ford:

If it is right and proper to help people to become wise managers of their own affairs in good times, it cannot be wrong to pursue the same object in dull times. Independence through self-dependence is a method which must commend itself when understood. Methods of self-help are numerous and great numbers of people have made the stimulating discovery that they need not depend on employers to find work for them—they can find work for themselves.[3]

And finding one's own work is, without doubt, one of the best ways to build up one's self-esteem and confidence and prove one's worth to the community. It is the ability to face and, with courage and diligence, overcome the most daunting hardships that separates people of true character and worth from the shiftless and worthless of society. Take, for instance, the powerful, inspiring testimony of commercial artist Harry Norgard, one of many millions of American workers who found themselves out of work in the early years of the Depression:

> I went out to free lance, find my own accounts. Within two months, I was making half again what I left. . . . I always felt deeply in my heart, you could always sell something if you offer the buyer something better than he's getting. It didn't matter to me whether there was a Depression or not. Bemoaning your fate gets you nowhere. I knew wherever you make an effort, you make headway. . . . The Depression [has] *made* a lot of people. I know one man who found himself out of work. He began thinking and thinking. He wrote sixteen letters to manufacturers and explained he could offer them a service at no cost. Three or four of them wrote back. In a few short years, he became an extremely wealthy man. He gave them something they needed, even though at the time they didn't know they needed it. . . . It never occurred to me to blame anybody but myself for what was happening to me. It would be the last thought to enter my mind.[4]

Salesman W. Clement Stone agrees, saying that "many of us [have] learned in the Depression how to turn a disadvantage into an advantage." One essential tool, he says, "is known as

PMA, positive mental attitude." Those with a negative mental attitude have only themselves to blame if they cannot find work; it is obvious that they lack a strong enough belief in their own abilities. Those with a strong PMA realize that opportunities are unlimited for anyone willing to work hard, insists Stone. "A person doesn't have to be poor. Anyone in the United States could acquire great wealth today."[5]

Even if we take Stone's last statement as an exaggeration and concede that substantial wealth is perhaps beyond the reach of every worker, making at least a comfortable living is certainly feasible for anyone with sufficient determination. A stunning example of people helping themselves is taking place in Pennsylvania's coal district. Teams of unemployed miners are digging small mines, trucking the coal to nearby cities, and selling it below the commercial rate. In this way, over twenty thousand men who might otherwise be standing in bread lines have, through a little ingenuity and a lot of determination and hard work, managed to support their families.[6]

Not everyone can find and mine coal, of course; but practically anyone can, during a pinch, make ends meet by working a piece of land. Henry Ford remarks that

> no unemployment insurance can be compared to an alliance between a man and a plot of land. . . . Let every man and every family at this season of the year cultivate a plot of land and raise a sufficient supply for themselves or others. Every city and village has vacant space whose use would be permitted. Groups of men could rent farms for small sums and operate them on the co-operative plan. Employed men, in groups of ten, twenty or fifty, could rent farms and operate them with several unemployed families. . . . Industrial concerns everywhere would gladly make it possible for their men, employed and unemployed, to find and work the land. Public-spirited citizens and institutions would most willingly assist in these efforts at self-help.[7]

Mr. Ford is right. Those who really need and want to work can find ways to do so, no matter how hard the times might be. There is no excuse for people who stand around doing nothing, their hands outstretched in hopes that the government will give them something for nothing. Harry Norgard hit the nail on the head when he said, "We are not all deserving the sympathy some of these bleeding hearts [liberals like FDR and his New Dealers] have for the people [who are unemployed and suffering]. A great deal of their misery is self-inflicted. These people are constantly looking for assistance. What would happen if we all had this attitude?"[8]

1. Quoted in Arthur M. Schlesinger Jr., *The Coming of the New Deal*. Boston: Houghton Mifflin, 1959, p. 275.

2. Herbert Hoover, "Press Statement of February 3, 1931," quoted in William S. Myers and Walter H. Newton, *The Hoover Administration: A Documented Narrative*. New York: Charles Scribner's Sons, 1936, pp. 63–64.

3. Henry Ford, "On Unemployment," *Literary Digest* (1932), in William Dudley, ed., *The Great Depression: Opposing Viewpoints*. San Diego: Greenhaven Press, 1994, pp. 41–44.

4. Quoted in Studs Terkel, *Hard Times: An Oral History of the Great Depression*. New York: Random House, 1970, pp. 439–41.

5. Quoted in Terkel, *Hard Times*, pp. 450–51.

6. See Howard Zinn, *A People's History of the United States*. New York: HarperCollins, 1980, pp. 385–86. Most of the miners involved dug on property owned by the companies that had laid them off. When company officials tried to prosecute the "bootleg" miners, local juries refused to convict them and local jailers refused to lock them up.

7. Ford, "On Unemployment," in Dudley, *The Great Depression*, p. 45.

8. Quoted in Terkel, *Hard Times*, p. 441.

"[When] there are so many people out of work that local funds are insufficient . . . it becomes the positive duty of the federal government to step in and help."

Self-Help Will Not Be Enough

Ideally speaking, self-reliance and self-help would be the best way for the millions of Americans presently unemployed to find work; however, the unfortunate truth is that we do not live in an ideal world. The suggestion much repeated of late by conservatives—that anyone who really wants work can find it if he or she is determined enough—is just plain wrong. In the first place, as President Roosevelt says, "Even in times of prosperity there are always some . . . people who want to work but can find no work."[1] Certainly in this present harrowing economic crisis, there are plenty of people who would give anything and have tried everything to find jobs.

Evidence for people's desire and willingness to work abounds. After visiting newly recruited CWA laborers in Iowa, for instance, journalist Lorena Hickok reported, "Did they want to work? In Sioux City they actually had fist fights over shovels!"[2] Joseph L. Heffernan, mayor of Youngstown, Ohio, during the early years of the Depression, tells of a seemingly endless stream of desperate citizens imploring him to give them jobs:

> One man I had known for years stood at my desk and calmly said, "My wife is frantic. After working at

the steel mill for twenty-five years, I have lost my job, and I'm too old to get other work. If you can't do something for me, I'm going to kill myself.". . . . To my home came a sad-eyed woman, the mother of nine children. No one in the family had had work in more than a year. . . . As time went on, business conditions showed no improvement. Every night hundreds of homeless men crowded into the municipal incinerator, where they found warmth even though they had to sleep on heaps of garbage.[3]

Mr. Heffernan's experience is not unique. Mayors across the country tell of thousands of people clamoring for jobs. People want to help themselves, all right. But when there are not enough jobs to go around, self-help is simply not enough; and that's when many have no choice but to turn to local charities and relief programs. Most of those forced to do so are not "lazy bums looking for a free handout," as some of the well-off are frequently heard to say. The vast majority are ashamed and embarrassed to have to turn to charity. "I have seen thousands of these defeated, discouraged, hopeless men and women," says Heffernan, "cringing and fawning as they come to ask for public aid. It is a spectacle of national degradation."[4] Take the individual case of clothes salesman Ben Isaacs:

We lost everything [when the Depression hit]. . . . I was going around trying to collect [earn] enough money to keep my family going. It was impossible. Very few people could pay you. Maybe a dollar if they would feel sorry for you. . . . I didn't want to go on relief. Believe me, when I was forced to go to the [relief] office . . . the tears were running out of my eyes. I couldn't bear myself to take the money from anybody for nothing. If it wasn't for those kids [of mine]—I tell you the truth—many a time it came to my mind to go commit suicide. . . . But somebody had to take care of those kids. . . . Wherever I went to get a job, I couldn't get no job. I went around

selling razor blades and shoe laces. There was a day
I would go over all the streets and come home with
fifty cents.[5]

Ben Isaacs's community relief center was one of the local
agencies President Hoover had touted as the solution to
unemployment and starvation. Inevitably, however, local
relief, equipped to help hundreds, has broken down under the
strain of trying to help thousands and millions. "We then
come," says Roosevelt, "to a situation where there are so many
people out of work that local funds are insufficient." It is then,
he adds, that it

> becomes the positive duty of the federal government
> to step in and help. In the words of our Democratic
> national platform, the federal government has a
> "continuous responsibility for human welfare, espe-
> cially for the protection of children." That duty and
> responsibility the federal government should carry
> out promptly, fearlessly and generously.[6]

Mr. Roosevelt's emphasis on helping children is a key point.
The failure of local relief hurts children the most; and the
children who are suffering the worst ravages of deprivation in
the present situation are going to be adversely emotionally
affected, perhaps for life. Today's children are tomorrow's
adults, who will inherit and have to deal with the society
shaped by today's adults. So when we neglect and brutalize
our children over some half-baked, outdated notion that the
federal government should stay out of people's lives, we are
doing nothing less than sabotaging the country's future.
According to Mr. Roosevelt:

> I cannot agree with the member of President
> Hoover's cabinet who suggests that this depression is
> not altogether a bad thing for our children. You and
> I know the appalling fact that malnutrition is one of
> the saddest by-products of unemployment. The
> health of these children is being affected not only

Many children lived in poverty during the Great Depression. Roosevelt stressed the government's responsibility to protect the welfare of the nation's children during this time of crisis.

now but for all the rest of their lives. Furthermore, a depression takes thousands of children away from schools and puts them to work to help the family income. They are underpaid and only too often work under conditions which, physically and morally, are often dangerous. It is well to remember, too, that the use of these untrained children in industry keeps many adults out of employment and has the effect of cutting down wages below a decent living standard.[7]

What, indeed, is the moral cost to children and adults alike of the federal government standing by and doing next to nothing, as it did when Mr. Hoover was in charge? Under normal conditions, the capability of people to help themselves, aided to a degree by local charity and relief efforts, would be enough to see the nation through hard times. But the conditions we face in this Depression are far beyond normal. They are, simply put, catastrophic. The fact is that the central government is the only agency with sufficient resources to create the huge number of jobs needed to reverse the present economic crisis. As Mr. Heffernan warns, if the government refuses to act, it will force millions of Americans to continue to demoralize themselves in their hopeless struggle for the dwindling scraps provided by increasingly overstrained charities and relief efforts. He says:

> Nobody has taken the trouble to weigh the consequences of our well-meant but ineffective charity upon the moral fiber of the American people. . . . We remain indifferent while millions of our fellow citizens are reduced to the status of paupers. . . . With quiet desperation they will bear hunger and mental anguish until every resource is exhausted. Then comes the ultimate struggle when, with heartache and an overwhelming sense of disgrace, they have to make the shamefaced journey to the door of public charity. This is the last straw. Their self-respect is destroyed. . . . That is the ultimate tragedy of America. If every mill and factory in the land should begin to hum with prosperity tomorrow morning, the destructive effect of our haphazard relief measures would not work itself out of the nation's blood until the sons of our sons have expiated the sins of our neglect.[8]

1. Franklin D. Roosevelt, "Radio Address on Unemployment and Social Welfare of October 13, 1932," quoted in Samuel I. Rosenman, ed., *The Public Papers and Addresses of Franklin D. Roosevelt*, Vol. 1. New York: Russell and Russell, 1969, p. 787.

2. Quoted in Arthur M. Schlesinger Jr., *The Coming of the New Deal*. Boston: Houghton Mifflin, 1959, p. 273.

3. Joseph L. Heffernan, "The Hungry City: A Mayor's Experience with Unemployment," in William Dudley, ed., *The Great Depression: Opposing Viewpoints*. San Diego: Greenhaven Press, 1994, pp. 34–35.

4. Heffernan, "The Hungry City," in Dudley, *The Great Depression*, p. 39.

5. Quoted in Studs Terkel, *Hard Times: An Oral History of the Great Depression*. New York: Random House, 1970, pp. 424–26.

6. Roosevelt, "Radio Address on Unemployment," in Rosenman, *Public Papers and Addresses*, Vol. 1, pp. 787, 789.

7. Roosevelt, "Radio Address on Unemployment," in Rosenman, *Public Papers and Addresses*, Vol. 1, pp. 792–93.

8. Heffernan, "The Hungry City," in Dudley, *The Great Depression*, pp. 38–39.

CHAPTER 2

Implementing the New Deal

"When we make one billionaire . . . we create an army of hungry children, ragged mothers, and broken-hearted fathers. We drag down our civilization to a point where, eventually, it must fail."

Redistribution of Wealth Offers a Way Out of the Depression

Author's Note: The essays in this chapter present opposing arguments over the impending implementation of New Deal programs and are therefore stated in the first person and the context of their time, namely the early to mid-1930s.

With millions of people out of work, many of them living in shanty towns and/or standing in bread lines, it is shameful that a tiny handful of extremely wealthy individuals and companies control and in a very real sense selfishly hoard most of the country's money. The shocking fact is that in the midst of the economic ravages of the Depression, the wealthy are actually getting wealthier. Journalist Edwin P. Hoyt reports that in 1933,

> while some people went hungry, and some actually starved, the income of corporations rose 35 percent . . . over the previous year, to $654,000,000. Individual incomes, however, dropped $340,000,000 in that same period. Even in this decrease, the rich

seemed to grow richer, while the poor languished. The number of people who earned $25,000 or more . . . *increased*, and their incomes increased, but those who earned less than $25,000 saw their incomes shrink, drastically and steadily. The number of persons who reported incomes of $1,000,000 or more jumped from twenty to forty-six.[1]

It would be much more equitable and humane if we could redistribute the wealth the nation produces so that even in hard times no one would suffer deprivation. As the popular senator from Louisiana, Huey P. Long, points out, no one is talking here about restricting the right of an individual to get rich. It's simply a matter of common fairness. "It is impossible," he maintains,

for the United States to preserve itself as a republic or as a democracy when 600 families own more of this nation's wealth—in fact, twice as much—as all the balance of the people put together. Ninety-six percent of our people live below the poverty line, while 4 percent own 87 percent of the wealth. America can have enough for all to live in comfort and still permit millionaires to own more than they can ever spend and to have more than they can ever use; but America cannot allow the multimillionaires and the billionaires, a mere handful of them, to own everything unless we are willing to inflict starvation upon 125,000,000 people.[2]

Huey Long

Indeed, the vast accumulations of wealth in the hands of an

elite few threatens to bring more than starvation; it foreshadows the destruction of the entire American way of life. George Norris, the well-known senator from Nebraska, inquires:

> Is there anything unjust or unfair that men of great wealth should be prohibited from passing on intact great fortunes which would result in such injury to society? When we make one billionaire, we make millions of paupers. Whenever a man is put in that class, we create an army of hungry children, ragged mothers, and broken-hearted fathers. We drag down our civilization to a point where, eventually, it must fail. If we would have a united country, we must have a country of homes. We must bring comfort and pleasure to the fireside. We must establish the home as the unit and in it must be maintained the comforts and pleasures of life. This can only come about if we prevent the accumulation of all the property in the hands of a few. Such a condition would, in the end, bring about a form of human slavery more bitter, more aggravated, and more heinous than any which have ever inflicted humanity.[3]

Should Wealth Be Shared?

Is "sharing the wealth," the catchphrase popularized by Senator Long, a desirable or even feasible goal? Evidently our national leaders think it is. In accepting the Democratic presidential nomination in 1932, Franklin D. Roosevelt declared, "Throughout the nation, men and women, forgotten in the political philosophy of the government of the last years, look to us here for guidance and for more equitable opportunity to share in the distribution of national wealth."[4] By "the government of the last years" Roosevelt meant, of course, Herbert Hoover's Republican administration. Yet it seems unfair to condemn the Republican leadership as uncaring to the plight of the poor. The fact is that Mr. Hoover himself advocated sharing the wealth during the 1932 campaign:

> My conception of America is a land where men and
> women may walk in ordered liberty, where they may
> enjoy the advantage of wealth not concentrated in
> the hands of a few but diffused through the lives of
> all, where they build and safeguard their homes
> [and] give to their children full opportunities of
> American life.[5]

It might be argued that these leaders from both parties do not
believe in their hearts that redistributing wealth in this country is possible; that they were, in the heat of a campaign sea-
son, merely telling the people what they wanted to hear. But
even if that is the case, it means at least that the politicians are
taking the nation's pulse and concluding that the majority of
Americans *do* want to hear this message. Clearly, the people
want a fairer apportioning of the plenty the country produces.

How, then, can we begin to redistribute the wealth?
Regardless of the feel-good political rhetoric, neither the
Democratic nor the Republican Party is thoroughly committed
and ready to do so on a large scale. Therefore, as the honorable
governor of Minnesota, Floyd B. Olson, has suggested, we may
need a third political party dedicated to creating a new and fairer economic system, one in which "wealth production is motivated by social needs." And this will only happen, he says,

> when the government actually takes over the impor-
> tant industries of the country. *A third party must arise
> and preach the gospel of government and collective owner-
> ship of the means of production and distribution.* . . . The
> platform of the third party must be based upon this
> vital economic issue. It must demand the taking of
> any and all steps necessary to guarantee human liber-
> ties and a decent standard of living. It must have an
> American concept based upon the rights of the peo-
> ple to "life, liberty and the pursuit of happiness."[6]

As for the specifics of economic redistribution, Senator
Long has laid out a tentative plan. He calls for government

allocation of a homestead allowance to all American families so that none would ever again fall below the poverty level. Moreover, the well-to-do would be allowed to amass only so much wealth—specifically, no more than 300 times the size of the average yearly family income. People over the age of sixty would receive pensions and the government would store surplus grain and other foodstuffs for free distribution during an emergency. In addition, the educational system would be expanded and improved so as to train more people for more and better jobs and to provide more equal opportunities for all. "The raising of revenue and taxes for the support of this program," says Long, should "come from the reduction of swollen fortunes from the top."[7] Surely, instituting such a just and humane plan would quickly end the Great Depression and ensure a brighter, more secure future for today's children and generations unborn.

1. Edwin P. Hoyt, *The Tempering Years*. New York: Charles Scribner's Sons, 1963, p. 80. To put these figures into some perspective, in 1933 the average American family earned between $600 and $1,200 per year; a family earning $3,000 per year could easily afford to own a home and a car; less than 1 percent of the nation's families earned $10,000 or higher per year; not surprisingly, then, a yearly income of $25,000 was considered a small fortune and $1 million or more per year a vast fortune.

2. Senator Huey P. Long, "Letter Published in the *Congressional Record* on May 23, 1935," quoted in William Dudley, ed., *The Great Depression: Opposing Viewpoints*. San Diego: Greenhaven Press, 1994, p. 149.

3. Senator George Norris, "Speech of February 15, 1935, to the University of Nebraska," quoted in Dudley, *The Great Depression*, p. 151.

4. Franklin D. Roosevelt, "Speech of July 2, 1932, to Democratic National Convention," quoted in Samuel I. Rosenman, ed., *The Public Papers and Addresses of Franklin D. Roosevelt*, Vol. 1. New York: Russell and Russell, 1969, p. 659.

5. Herbert Hoover, "Speech of October 31, 1932, at Madison Square Garden," quoted in William S. Myers and Walter H. Newton, *The Hoover Administration: A Documented Narrative*. New York: Charles Scribner's Sons, 1936, p. 521.

6. Floyd B. Olson, "My Political Creed," *Common Sense* (1935), quoted in Howard Zinn, ed., *New Deal Thought*. Indianapolis: Bobbs-Merrill Company, 1966, p. 397.

7. Long, "Letter of May 23, 1935," in Dudley, *The Great Depression*, p. 153.

"Confiscation of wealth may satisfy the vengeful in us. It may soothe a retaliatory spirit. But it is the path of national suicide."

Redistribution of Wealth Will Hurt Instead of Help

The often-heard cry of "sharing the wealth," of redistributing the country's earned income in efforts to alleviate the Depression in particular and poverty in general, is both cheap political rhetoric and a practical sham. It is rhetoric because no politician with any brains would seriously consider destroying the profit system that has made America the richest country on earth. The fact is that even in the midst of the present economic crisis, the worst on record, our nation is better off than any of its global neighbors; and any major attempt to redistribute wealth would only deepen the worldwide Depression by destroying the profit motive of those who control production and supply most of the jobs. What incentive would truly motivated and industrious people have to achieve and to strive for excellence if the government took away their hard-earned money and gave it, free of charge, to those less motivated and industrious? According to journalist and social commentator David Lawrence:

> [If] we are seriously examining an uneven distribution of worldly goods, we must find some way to

retain all the incentive of the profit system—for otherwise the government credit will collapse through lack of revenues—and yet remove all the abuses which permit men to exploit their fellow men. . . . If we enforce the laws against fraud and dishonesty, if we prevent exploitation of human labor or sweatshop conditions, or the payment of wages below a decent standard of living, we will have attained through government a social advance highly desirable. But there is no reason why such steps should require the destruction of the profit system.[1]

Besides the collapse of revenue and credit, a wealth redistribution system poses other potential dangers to the nation. First, in order to implement such a system, the government would have to begin large-scale economic planning; in short, it would have to collectivize, or control and direct, major industries. This would be ominously similar to the communist social order imposed on Russia by the Bolsheviks after World War I, which is clearly an antidemocratic system that discourages personal incentives to work hard and get ahead. As popular columnist Walter Lippmann states it:

A plan for production is incompatible with voluntary labor, with freedom to choose an occupation. A plan of production is not only a plan of consumption, but a plan of how long and where the people shall work, and what they shall work at. By no possible manipulation of wage rates could the planners attract to the various jobs precisely the right number of workers. Under voluntary labor, particularly with consumption rationed and standardized, the unpleasant jobs would be avoided and the good jobs overcrowded. Therefore the inevitable and necessary complement of the rationing of consumption is the conscription of labor, either by overt act or law or by driving workers into the undesirable jobs by offering them starvation as the alternative.[2]

Such a plan would have the harmful potential not only of blunting freedom and initiative for the general population, but also of consolidating enormous power in the hands of a few, the very thing that share-the-wealth advocates want to avoid. In a government-controlled economic system, who will decide what and how much gets produced, as well as who works at what job? "The idea of economic planning," warns respected philosopher-scholar Robert M. MacIver, "may be tied up to the principle of economic nationalism—a danger of which there have already been significant signs—or even of economic imperialism."[3] Thus, when the profit system, imperfect as it may be, is undermined, we should not be surprised to find ourselves living under the thumb of a dictator.

Still another downside of a wholesale redistribution of wealth would be an almost inevitable and severe reduction of philanthropy and charity, of the spirit that moves those who have plenty to give to those who have little or nothing. Again, this would work directly against the goals of those who want to eliminate poverty. Lawrence points out that when the economic system is upset, the common people are the first to suffer. He explains:

> The sad truth will be confirmed by any social welfare worker who tries to raise funds for a hospital. Where are the rich of yesterday? Who can be found to give as generously as some who have been swept into oblivion and into the humiliating bankruptcies that have [wiped out] wealth from coast to coast? Where are the philanthropically inclined who gave ungrudgingly only two or three years ago to their colleges, their schools, to recreational centers for the poor, to the jobless in the first year or so of the Depression? . . . Giving will never again in this generation be America's greatest attribute. The people collectively used to average gifts of about two billion dollars a year to philanthropic causes. This will not come again because the government has taken over involuntarily

Unemployed men in Chicago receive a free meal at a charity soup kitchen in this 1930 photograph. During the Great Depression, many charities and philanthropists came to the aid of the poor.

the task of providing the social improvements which private philanthropy used to furnish.[4]

All of these arguments presuppose that a massive wealth redistribution program would actually end up putting money in the pockets of those who need it. But the best and most widely endorsed such program suggested to date, the "Share the Wealth" plan of Louisiana's Senator Huey P. Long, is, despite its pie-in-the-sky promises, plainly unworkable. W.B. Bell, president of the American Cyanamid Company, has analyzed Long's program in detail and concludes that when the total moneys taken from the rich are divided among thirty million or so families, the share per family will end up being very tiny. Bell reports:

> Senator Long proposes to give each of us a home worth a minimum of $5,000, together with all the desired home comforts, by stripping those who have fortunes of more than $2,500,000 of all in excess of that sum. But this initial distribution of wealth works out [to be] much less per person [than Long claims]. It would not yield the $5,000 home, with or without the comforts. . . . Those of us who would benefit by the operation would hope to receive on the average, at most, about $135. . . . Furthermore, our industrial and economic system would not within the lifetime of any of those here present recover from such a blow to initiative, energy, thrift and ambition. . . . Huey Long's "Share the Wealth" plan is impracticable and won't work.[5]

Senator Long has skillfully tapped into the envy and resentment that poor people often feel for the rich. It is only natural and right to desire and work toward an ideal society in which no one wants or suffers; but robbing the most industrious and fortunate Americans of their hard-earned goods will not only fail to enrich others, but in the process destroy the American system. As Lawrence aptly puts it, "Confiscation of wealth may satisfy the vengeful in us. It may soothe a retaliatory spirit. But it is the path of national suicide."[6]

1. David Lawrence, *Beyond the New Deal*. New York: McGraw-Hill, 1934, p. 135.

2. Walter Lippmann, "Planning for Peace in an Economy of Abundance," in *The Good Society*. Boston: Little, Brown, 1937, p. 102.

3. Robert M. MacIver, "Social Philosophy," quoted in Howard Zinn, ed., *New Deal Thought*. Indianapolis: Bobbs-Merrill Company, 1966, p. 62.

4. Lawrence, *Beyond the New Deal*, pp. 138–39.

5. W.B. Bell, "Speech of July 29, 1935, to University of Virginia Institute of Public Affairs," quoted in William Dudley, ed., *The Great Depression: Opposing Viewpoints*. San Diego: Greenhaven Press, 1994, p. 158.

6. Lawrence, *Beyond the New Deal*, p. 144.

"[Social security] will discourage and defeat the American trait of thrift. It will go a long way toward destroying American initiative and courage. No man can determine with any degree of accuracy its cost upon the present or future generation."

Social Security Will Not Benefit America

The Social Security Act, primarily designed to provide Americans with old-age pensions, is a badly thought-out, disorganized, ineffective, and potentially harmful plan and should not be allowed to continue. Supposedly, it will help in the country's financial recovery, as well as "lessen the force of possible future depressions." Thus, claims President Roosevelt, the program, in conjunction with some of his other New Deal efforts, "will take care of human needs and at the same time provide for the United States an economic structure of vastly greater soundness."[1] Yet, as John C. Gall, of the National Association of Manufacturers, asks:

> How can recovery be promoted by additional expenditures from a federal treasury already far in the red? How can recovery be promoted by the levy of new and additional taxes on employers and employees, when the effect is to draw from the channels of trade and commerce a substantial portion of the income normally spent for goods and services?[2]

Gall and other responsible business leaders agree that the answer to these questions is that Social Security *cannot* help the nation recover from the economic crisis it presently faces. First, in its attempt to plan ahead to alleviate *future* unemployment, the program does not address *today's* severe unemployment problems. Second, as Mr. Gall has just mentioned, Social Security gets its funding by collecting "contributions"—a sugarcoated way of saying "taxes"—from both employers and employees. This means that in the midst of hard times, when employers desperately need to increase profits and employees just as desperately need higher wages, both are forced to pay more out of their pockets. And for what? For the promise, say the program's advocates, that when they grow old, they will get some of that money back. But will they? We must concede the very real possibility that some future session of Congress may decide to cancel the program; such a move would wipe out these supposed pensions and it would then be too late for those who had already contributed to get their money back.

This raises the question of how thoughtfully and solidly the Social Security bill was written in the first place. Close scrutiny reveals it was hastily and haphazardly thrown together. No one knows or articulates this better than Raymond Moley, formerly of Columbia University. Originally the most important member of Roosevelt's "brain trust," the group of liberal academics who assist him at policy making and speech writing, Mr. Moley, has understandably become disillusioned with the extreme measures the New Deal has perpetrated and continues to perpetrate on the American people. Recalling the development of the Social Security bill, Moley states:

> To prepare the [bill], the president had set up a Cabinet Committee. This Committee then established a research organization and asked a considerable number of citizens, including myself, to serve as an advisory committee. The advisory committee considered every aspect of the problem with care and

made a series of recommendations to the Cabinet Committee, which promptly threw out many of them. The bill that was finally sent to Congress was so largely the result of an attempt to compromise irreconcilable views that frank observers recognized it for the mess it was. . . . Quite clearly, the legislation should have been delayed for another year. The Act, as finally passed, has gross defects.[3]

Social Security's shaky conception and lack of effectiveness are not its only or, for that matter, its worst defects. The program is also potentially harmful because it, like so many other left-wing New Deal schemes, promotes un-American values, such as laziness and complacency. Daniel O. Hastings, the distinguished Republican senator from Delaware, fears

that when the federal government undertakes the job of social security, through direct taxation for that purpose, it has taken a step that can hardly be retraced. I fear it may end the progress of a great country and bring its people to the level of the average European. It will . . . add great strength to the political demagogue. It will assist in driving worthy and courageous men from public life. It will discourage and defeat the American trait of thrift. It will go a long way toward destroying American initiative and courage. No man can determine with any degree of accuracy its cost upon the present or future generation. There is danger of our sympathy for its humane objectives overcoming our mature judgment.[4]

James L. Donnelly, of the Illinois Manufacturers' Association, agrees, saying that Social Security will undermine our national way of life "by destroying initiative, discouraging thrift, and stifling individual responsibility."[5]

Indeed, the word *Social* in the bill's title is not misplaced, for the program is clearly a giant step in the direction of socialism, of the government controlling people's lives from the cradle to the grave. As the National Association of

Library of Congress

Manufacturers states, it will facilitate "ultimate socialistic control of life and industry." One prominent congressman has warned that over time, as new generations are enslaved and exploited by the system, "the lash of the dictator will be felt." And mirroring this worry, another congressman, James W. Wadsworth of New York, comments, "This bill opens the door and invites the entrance into the political field of a power so vast, so powerful as to threaten the integrity of our institutions and to pull the pillars of the temple down upon the heads of our descendants."[6]

In all likelihood, such dire predictions thankfully will not come to pass, since it is quite possible that Social Security will, in the very near future, collapse of its own weight; for in creating this vast social welfare program, the federal government may be tampering in the states' domain; and therefore, it may be unconstitutional. Ironically, when still governor of New York, Mr. Roosevelt implied rather forcefully that the central government lacks a constitutional right to meddle with programs traditionally run by the states. He said:

> As a matter of fact and law, the governing rights of the states are all of those which have not been surrendered to the national government by the Constitution or its amendments. Wisely or unwisely, people know that under the Eighteenth Amendment Congress has been given the right to legislate on this particular subject, but this is not the case in the matter of a great number of other vital problems of government, such as the conduct of public utilities, of banks, of insurance, of business, of agriculture, of education, of *social welfare* and a dozen other important features. In these, Washington must *not* be encouraged to interfere."[7] [emphases added]

If the federal government must not interfere in social welfare endeavors, why is it doing so now in implementing the Social Security program? The answer is that Roosevelt speaks out of both sides of his mouth. Social Security is misguided, destructive of good values, and of questionable legality; it should be eliminated before it does any serious damage to the nation.

1. Franklin D. Roosevelt, "Presidential Statement upon Signing the Social Security Act, August 14, 1935," in Samuel I. Rosenman, ed., *The Public Papers and Addresses of Franklin D. Roosevelt*, Vol. 4. New York: Russell and Russell, 1969, p. 324.

2. John C. Gall, "Will the Administration's Social Security Bill Promote Recovery?" Radio speech of June 6, 1935, quoted in William Dudley, ed., *The Great Depression: Opposing Viewpoints*. San Diego: Greenhaven Press, 1994, p. 171.

3. Raymond Moley, *After Seven Years*. New York: Harper and Brothers, 1939, p. 303.

4. Quoted in Dudley, *The Great Depression*, p. 171.

5. Quoted in Arthur M. Schlesinger Jr., *The Coming of the New Deal*. Boston: Houghton Mifflin, 1959, p. 311.

6. Quoted in Schlesinger, *The Coming of the New Deal*, pp. 311–12.

7. Roosevelt, "Radio Address of March 2, 1930, on States' Rights," in Rosenman, *Public Papers and Addresses*, Vol. 1, p. 569. Roosevelt here refers to the Eighteenth Amendment, prohibiting the manufacture, sale, and transportation of alcoholic beverages, which was ratified in 1919. In 1920 Congress passed the Volstead Act, providing for enforcement of the amendment. Because Prohibition, as it came to be called, proved ineffective, with rampant violations on all social levels, it was repealed by the Twenty-First Amendment in 1933.

"Our social security program will be a vital force working against the recurrence of severe depressions in the future. . . . It will make this great republic a better and a happier place in which to live—for us, our children and our children's children."

Social Security Will Benefit America

The passage of the Social Security Act of 1935 constitutes a constructive landmark in the ongoing legislative evolution of our great democratic nation. As President Roosevelt has recently stated, it is the "supreme achievement of this great Congress," and "in days to come will provide the aged against distressing want, will set up a national system of insurance for the unemployed, and . . . extend well-merited care to sick and crippled children."[1] The president, his secretary of labor, Frances Perkins, and the Congress should be congratulated for pushing through a bill sorely needed and long overdue.[2]

For too long, the aged and infirm in our society, especially those lacking the aid of relatives or friends, have suffered deprivation because they could no longer earn enough money to get by. And for the most part, government's answer to their plight has been constantly to recite the cold and pitiless creed of rugged individualism and self-reliance. "You should have been more frugal and saved for your old age," goes the tired refrain. "Hardworking people do not owe a living to those who fail to work hard and plan ahead." The movement for old-age pensions began in earnest around the turn of the century with the lobbying efforts of Isaac M. Rubinow's American Association of Labor Legislation. And in 1924 the American Association of Old Age Security, founded by Abraham Epstein, joined the battle. These groups relentlessly pushed individual state governments to enact old-age legislation until they achieved their first major victory—passage of the New York State's Old Age Security Act of 1930, signed by then-governor Franklin Roosevelt.

The forces of decency and fair play scored a much greater victory when President Roosevelt recently signed the national Social Security Act. Frances Perkins here explains some of what the new legislation entails:

> This act establishes unemployment insurance as a substitute for haphazard methods of assistance in periods when men and women willing and able to work are without jobs. It provides for old age pensions . . . for those who have been unable to provide for the years when they no longer can work. It also provides security for dependent and crippled children, mothers, the indigent disabled and the blind. . . . Old-age benefits in the form of monthly payments are to be paid to individuals who have worked and contributed to the insurance fund in direct proportion to the total wages earned by such individuals in the course of their employment. . . . The minimum monthly payment is to be $10, the maximum $85. These payments will begin in the year 1942 and will be to those who have worked and contributed. . . . As an example of the practical operation of the old-age benefit system, consider for a moment a typical young man of thirty-five years of age, and let us compute the benefits which will accrue to him. Assuming that his income will average $100 per month over the period of thirty years until he reaches the age of sixty-five, the benefit payments due him . . . will provide him with

> $42.50 per month for the remainder of his life. . . .
> In the event that death occurs prior to the age of
> sixty-five, 3½% of the total wages earned by him . . .
> will be returned to his dependents.[3]

The Social Security Act is certainly not meant as a panacea and plainly will not help all needy people all of the time. As the president said when signing the act into law on August 14, 1935:

> We can never insure one hundred percent of the
> population against one hundred percent of the haz-
> ards . . . of life, but we have tried to frame a law
> which will give some measure of protection to the
> average citizen and to his family against the loss of a
> job and against poverty-ridden old age.[4]

This "measure of protection" is meant as a supplement to, rather than as the sole substance of, an elderly person's yearly income. Naturally, then, people will still need to be thrifty and save and invest as much as they can in their working years. This shows how groundless are the claims made by opponents of the act—that people will become lazy and spendthrift in expectation of the government giving them a free ride later. As Secretary Perkins's figures reveal, the monthly payments proposed are very low—barely enough to live on in most cases—so there clearly will be no such free ride.

Nor, for that matter, is there anything at all *free* about the proposed monthly payments. The act will be regularly fund-ed by contributions made by wage earners and their employ-ers. The employers will surely make up for these outlays by charging a bit more for their products, so their profit line will not suffer; and their employees, partly through buying these products and partly through the deductions from their wages, will, in effect, little by little create their own pensions. Since the government will neither financially support anyone nor force anyone to work at a particular job (or to work at all, if that is their choice), this can scarcely be described as social-ism, as the act's opponents often claim.

In fact, far from being too extreme, many people feel that Social Security's main flaw is that it does not go far enough in helping those most in need and that it should, therefore, be expanded over time. Congressman Henry Ellenbogen of Pennsylvania contends:

> Old-age pensions, as provided for in the Social Security Act, are but the foundation for a real set-up of old-age security in America. To my mind, these provisions of the act should be, and I hope in time will be, much more liberal and generous than they are now. . . . We now have the foundation; we can improve and enlarge from time to time the building which we construct upon that foundation.[5]

In particular, Mr. Ellenbogen objects to the age limit now set on retirement. "The 65-year limit in the federal bill must go," he asserts.

> It is entirely too high. After all, this is supposed to be a pension for old age, not a graveyard pension. Most people who are 60 years of age are old—the years ahead of them hold no prospect of jobs or gainful occupation. They have every right to live their last years in comfort, in economic peace and security.[6]

A Fair and Workable System

Perhaps sometime in the future Congress will see fit to lower the retirement age and/or improve the system in other ways. At least for the present, a fair and workable system at last exists, one that is good for the country and that the vast majority of the people strongly favor. As Secretary Perkins astutely comments:

> This is truly legislation in the interest of the national welfare. We must recognize that if we are to maintain a healthy economy and thriving production, we need to maintain the standard of living of the lower income groups of our population who constitute

ninety percent of our purchasing power. . . . Our social security program will be a vital force working against the recurrence of severe depressions in the future. We can, as the principle of sustained purchasing power in hard times makes itself felt in every shop, store and mill, grow old without being haunted by the specter of a poverty-ridden old age or of being a burden on our children. . . . The American people want such security as the law provides. It will make this great republic a better and a happier place in which to live—for us, our children and our children's children.[7]

1. Franklin D. Roosevelt, "Address of November 27, 1935, in Atlanta, Georgia," in Samuel I. Rosenman, ed., *The Public Papers and Addresses of Franklin D. Roosevelt*, Vol. 4. New York: Russell and Russell, 1969, p. 472.

2. Frances Perkins (1882–1965), who served as secretary of labor from 1933 to 1945, was the first woman U.S. cabinet member. She worked tirelessly for social legislation, including—besides social security—minimum wages, maximum working hours, and the abolition of child labor. Her widely read book, *The Roosevelt I Knew* (New York: Harper and Row, 1946), reveals much about the inner workings of the New Deal and the beliefs of those who shaped it.

3. Frances Perkins, "The Social Security Act" (1935), quoted in William E. Leuchtenburg, ed., *The New Deal: A Documentary History*. New York: Harper and Row, 1968, pp. 81–82.

4. Franklin D. Roosevelt, "Presidential Statement upon Signing the Social Security Act, August 14, 1935," in Rosenman, *Public Papers and Addresses*, Vol. 4, p. 324.

5. Quoted in Howard Zinn, ed., *New Deal Thought*. Indianapolis: Bobbs-Merrill Company, 1966, pp. 284, 290.

6. Quoted in Zinn, *New Deal Thought*, p. 284.

7. Perkins, "The Social Security Act," in Leutchenburg, *The New Deal*, pp. 85–86.

"[President Roosevelt's] administration of relief, in which Negroes have received the same consideration as whites, has given the members of the Negro race a standing which they have not enjoyed since they became citizens."

Blacks Are Benefiting from the New Deal

Author's note: This viewpoint and the one that follows quote material from the 1930s, when American blacks were commonly referred to as "Negroes" and "colored" people, neither of which was then considered a derogatory term.

In the opening few years of Franklin Roosevelt's New Deal, American blacks have made more economic and social gains than in all of the preceding presidential administrations since the Civil War combined. President Roosevelt, states the distinguished secretary of the interior Harold L. Ickes,

> has realized, as no other president since Lincoln seemed to realize, that the mere existence in the federal Constitution of the 13th, 14th and 15th amendments [which granted blacks freedom, citizenship, and voting rights] is no guarantee of their enforcement. Among his many humane and far-sighted acts has been that of a vigorous policy of justice toward Negroes. His administration of relief, in which Negroes have received the same consideration as whites, has given the members of the Negro race a

standing which they have not enjoyed since they became citizens.[1]

By contrast, President Hoover, while claiming blacks were well-off under his leadership, did virtually nothing to improve their lives. "The greatest single factor in the progress of the Negro race has been the schools," Hoover stated in April 1931, "established and conducted by high-minded, self-sacrificing men and women of both races and all sections of the country."[2] Yet black schools, especially in the South, remained few and grossly substandard under the Hoover administration. In addition, Mr. Hoover refused to condemn the lynching of blacks, which occurred at least fifty-seven times during his term; nominated for the Supreme Court a Southern judge who had publicly called for taking away blacks' voting rights; and refused to be photographed with blacks until the last month of his second presidential campaign.

Since taking office in 1933, President Roosevelt and his closest associates have sought to treat black Americans more fairly, more equally, and with more dignity. They have found this effort to be a difficult uphill battle, mainly because of the deeply ingrained racism that pervades the country, especially in the South. In setting up the Public Works Administration (PWA), Mr. Ickes officially ordered that there be "no discrimination exercised against any person because of color or religious affiliation."[3] Unfortunately, despite this admonition, some discrimination has occurred on PWA projects, as well as in other New Deal programs; but the blame for this must be placed on existing prejudice, not on the New Deal or its administrators, who have struggled earnestly against such prejudice. As Ickes himself has cautioned, "The prejudices that have been fostered and built up for 60 years cannot be done away with over night."[4]

Noted journalist Edwin P. Hoyt here describes part of the enormous load of prejudice that blacks face and the New Deal seeks to remedy:

Negroes [have] secured a special justice in America—harsher than the justice meted out to whites. They [have] performed the same work alongside white workers, and received less pay for it. They [have been] the last hired and the first fired. Few Negroes [have taken] any interest in education or self-improvement because they [have] learned from painful experience that no matter how much they exercise their brains, there [is] a low ceiling of accomplishment for Negroes in the white community.[5]

Harold Ickes agrees, adding:

In the exercise of the suffrage that is guaranteed him by the Constitution the Negro has met with many abuses and obstacles. In some localities he is callously disfranchised; in other places, for generations, he has been exploited by corrupt politicians, who have bought his vote or have made him promises which were never expected to be kept.[6]

Most powerful and disturbing of all is the testimony of blacks like Nate Shaw, an Alabama cotton farmer, who tells of conditions that all his life have "been outrageous every way you can think against the colored race of people." America has long been a white man's world, says Shaw, and the "colored man just been a dog for this country for years and years."[7]

Yet in spite of this seemingly overwhelming obstacle of deeply rooted prejudice and the difficulties Roosevelt and his New Dealers have had in battling it, they must be credited with making some significant headway. According to University of Delaware scholar Raymond Wolters, the New Deal has "offered Negroes more in material benefits and recognition than [has] any administration since the era of Reconstruction."[8] Several New Deal programs, including the PWA and CCC (Civilian Conservation Corps), have become, in effect, instruments of social justice by paying blacks the same wages as whites for the same work. Demonstrating that this marks a major change from the past is the fact that many whites, particularly in the South, have loudly complained about such equal treatment. Not long ago, Georgia's governor, Eugene Talmadge, forwarded to President Roosevelt a letter from a "good, honest, hard-working" white farmer, saying:

> All our Negro farm labor that we used to farm with are sitting around town, waiting for a ditch [digging] job [for the PWA] at $1.30 a day. They prefer this to working for a farmer at farm wages, the general price of which seems to be 40 to 50 cents a day. . . . I can't blame them. I wouldn't plow nobody's mule from sunrise to sunset for 50 cents a day when I could get $1.30 for pretending to work on a ditch.[9]

Though unstated, the real meaning of this complaint is that Roosevelt's programs are upsetting the "natural way of things," in which blacks' primary purpose in life is to supply cheap labor for whites. Mr. Roosevelt's response: "I take it . . . that you approve of farm labor at forty to fifty cents per day. . . . Somehow I cannot get it into my head that wages on such a scale make possible a reasonable American standard of living."[10] True to his word, the president has made it possible for many blacks to achieve a reasonable living standard. The CCC, for example, has put over 200,000 blacks to work, thereby helping many to get a decent start in life; and, courageously ignoring the complaints of racist governors and legislators, the president has put a number of blacks in positions of authority at the CCC, including 39 reserve officers and 152 educational advisers.

In addition to putting many blacks to work at decent wages, the government has erected numerous public facilities for blacks that otherwise would never have been built. In Mr. Roosevelt's first term alone, the PWA spent more than $13,000,000 on black schools and hospitals, far more than had been spent in the entire seven decades since the end of the Civil War. And blacks now live in one-third of the 140,000 housing units constructed by the PWA, even though they make up less than 10 percent of the population. These are just a few of the many examples of how the Roosevelt administration has benefited and will no doubt continue to benefit black Americans. As an editorial in the *Pittsburgh Courier* accurately states it, thanks to the New Deal:

A poster advertises the "Colored Concert Band," a group sponsored by the Works Progress Administration. The government sponsored artistic as well as construction projects.

armies of unemployed Negro workers have been kept from the near starvation level on which they lived under President Hoover. . . . Armies of unemployed Negro workers have found work on the various PWA, CWA, WPA, CCC . . . and other projects. . . . Critics will point to [various examples of] discrimination [occurring in these programs]. . . . This is all true. . . . But what administration within the memory of man has done a better job in that direction? . . . The answer, of course, is none.[11]

1. Harold L. Ickes, "The Negro as a Citizen," *The Crisis* (1936), quoted in Howard Zinn, ed., *New Deal Thought.* Indianapolis: Bobbs-Merrill Company, 1966, pp. 342–43.

2. Herbert Hoover, "Address of April 14, 1931, commemorating the anniversary of the founding of Tuskegee Institute," quoted in William S. Myers and Walter H. Newton, *The Hoover Administration: A Documented Narrative.* New York: Charles Scribner's Sons, 1936, p. 474.

3. Quoted in Raymond Wolters, "The New Deal and the Negro," in John Braeman et al., eds., *The New Deal: The National Level.* Columbus: Ohio State University Press, 1975, p. 187.

4. Ickes, "The Negro as a Citizen," in Zinn, *New Deal Thought*, p. 343.

5. Edwin P. Hoyt, *The Tempering Years.* New York: Charles Scribner's Sons, 1963, p. 117.

6. Ickes, "The Negro as a Citizen," in Zinn, *New Deal Thought*, p. 341.

7. Quoted in Theodore Rosengarten, *All God's Dangers: The Life of Nate Shaw.* New York: Knopf, 1974, pp. 299–300.

8. Wolters, "The New Deal and the Negro," in Braeman et al., *The New Deal*, p. 170.

9. Quoted in Ted Morgan, *FDR: A Biography.* New York: Simon and Schuster, 1985, p. 418.

10. Quoted in Morgan, *FDR*, p. 418. The president did not end up mailing his strongly worded reply to Governor Talmadge, mainly for fear of alienating the leader of the state where Roosevelt's Warm Springs Foundation (an international center for the study and treatment of polio, with which he was afflicted) was located.

11. *Pittsburgh Courier*, January 11, 1936, quoted in Braeman et al., *The New Deal*, pp. 210–11.

"The [New Deal's] philosophy seems to be that once the Depression is over and the economy has revived, blacks should be expected, as a group, to return to their dismal status at the bottom of the social-economic ladder."

Blacks Are Not Benefiting from the New Deal

The Roosevelt administration claims it is helping American blacks to overcome prejudice and to better themselves. Yet in every New Deal program instituted so far, black workers have suffered blatant discrimination, humiliation, and unwarranted firings, while white workers have received clear preferential treatment. No one can deny that deep-rooted racism pervades the nation, creating a cruel and formidable barrier against upward social mobility for black citizens. But when they took office, the president and his chief assistants promised to do something about this deplorable state of affairs. "Negroes are demanding that the ideals and principles upon which the nation was founded shall be translated into action," said Harold Ickes, secretary of the interior and director of the PWA (Public Works Administration). "Your government at the present time," he told black citizens, "is not insensitive to [your plight], for . . . it is attempting to build a new social order and to set up higher ideals for all of its citizens."[1] The New Deal having been in place for several years now,

American blacks have every right to ask when this "new social order" is finally going to arrive. So far, for them, it has not.

The evidence for the failure of the New Deal to help American blacks is overwhelming. The misuse of moneys belonging to black citizens in the implementation of the Agricultural Adjustment Administration (AAA) constitutes just one example. This program was designed to raise the prices of farm products by persuading farmers to grow fewer crops; the AAA disbursed government benefit payments to those farmers who promised to cultivate only a portion of their acreage. The problem is that most black farmers, especially in the South, are tenants working land owned by whites. According to AAA rules, the landlord and tenant are supposed to split the benefit payment fifty-fifty; however, across the South, white landlords have been shafting their tenants, giving them one-sixth, one-tenth, or even none of the payment.

And white owners and public officials have used other illegal means of robbing poor blacks of their fair share of AAA benefits, as well as moneys from various relief programs. University of North Carolina sociologist Guy Johnson reports:

> Negro tenants received pitifully little of the crop reduction money last fall. [White] landlords quite generally took charge of the checks and applied them to back debts of the tenants. Furthermore, many landlords are known to have "understandings" with local relief administrators to prevent the "demoralization" of their Negro labor, and it is reported that some go so far as to charge their tenants' accounts all food and other supplies furnished by the relief office. The director of relief in a southern seaboard city remarked not long ago, "I don't like this fixing of a wage scale for work relief. Why, the niggers in this town are getting so spoiled working on these relief jobs at thirty cents an hour that they won't work on the docks for fifty cents a day like they did last year."[2]

What is more, whites have made sure that the wording of AAA-overseen contracts for cotton, production of which employs more blacks than any other single crop, allows landlords to evict those tenants whom they deem "unneeded" due to the program's crop reductions. The results have been predictable. Over a hundred thousand black tenant farmers and their families have been evicted since the New Deal was implemented. Clearly, AAA officials and the leaders of Roosevelt's relief efforts are fully aware of these unfair practices but have done next to nothing to stop them.

Neither has the present government done anything about blatant discrimination in the operation of three of its most ambitious and highly touted programs—the National Recovery Administration

Critics of the Roosevelt administration contend that black tenant farmers were deprived of an equal share of federal aid through the New Deal and thus remained in poverty.

(NRA), Civilian Conservation Corps (CCC), and Tennessee Valley Authority (TVA). These agencies are supposedly designed to stimulate the economy, the NRA by regulating commerce and labor in a fair and even manner, and the CCC and TVA by putting unemployed people back to work. The fair-wage guidelines the NRA forced on American businesses may have been well-meaning and probably did help some white workers; but they actually harmed numerous black workers, who were the first to be laid off when factories modernized. Historian Raymond Wolters cites a typical example in Greensboro, Georgia:

> Twenty Negroes were employed by a cotton textile mill. Before the NRA, the daily wages of workers at

the mill was about 75 cents for a ten-hour day; afterward, wages ranged from $2 to $2.40 for an eight-hour day. The machinery in the mill was obsolete, and the firm had been able to compete with modernized mills only because its labor costs were so low. With the coming of the NRA, the mill had only two viable alternatives: to evade the NRA's stipulations . . . or to install more productive machinery and pay code wages to fewer workers. . . . The mill made the second choice. After the new machines were installed, the management calculated that the mill could produce the same amount of goods with twenty fewer workers, and the Negroes were released.[3]

The CCC has admittedly provided jobs for many black Americans. But the agency has also carefully segregated nearly all of them from their white coworkers in separate housing camps. CCC leaders have also seen to it that blacks in the program receive very limited educational/skills training, slanting what they do receive toward preparation for menial, low-paying jobs. The program's philosophy seems to be that once the Depression is over and the economy has revived, blacks should be expected, as a group, to return to their dismal status at the bottom of the social-economic ladder. If the CCC and other New Deal programs are indeed the "instruments of social justice" their creators claim them to be, they should be vigorously preparing blacks and other disadvantaged minorities to move up the ladder. As scholar John Salmond puts it, "The failure of CCC [is] not so much one of performance as of potential. Much [has] been accomplished, but much more could conceivably [be] done."[4]

Discrimination against blacks is even worse in the TVA, contends black writer John P. Davis, a frequent critic of Roosevelt's policies. Like other New Deal programs, Davis says, the TVA operates "in callous disregard of the interdiction in the Constitution of the United States against use of federal funds for projects which discriminate against applicants solely on the ground of color."[5] Maintaining a "lily-white" policy, TVA officials have excluded blacks from living in Norris, Tennessee, a model town built to house the workers on Norris Dam. Moreover, Davis points out,

> the [TVA's] payroll of Negro workers remains disproportionately lower than that of whites. While the government has maintained a trade school to train workers on the project, no Negro trainees have been admitted. Nor have any meaningful plans matured for the future of the . . . Negro workers who in another year or so will be left without employment, following completion of work on the dams being built by TVA. . . . None of the officials of TVA seems to have the remotest idea of how Negroes in the Tennessee Valley will be able to buy the cheap electricity which TVA is designed to produce.[6]

These instances of bold-faced inequities and discrimination in New Deal programs show quite clearly that the Roosevelt administration's promises to aid suffering blacks have been cruelly misleading and false.

1. Harold L. Ickes, "The Negro as a Citizen," *The Crisis* (1936), quoted in Howard Zinn, ed., *New Deal Thought*. Indianapolis: Bobbs-Merrill Company, 1966, pp. 343–44.

2. Guy B. Johnson, "Does the South Owe the Negro a New Deal?" *Social Forces* (1934), quoted in Zinn, *New Deal Thought*, p. 311.

3. Raymond Wolters, "The New Deal and the Negro," in John Braeman et al., eds., *The New Deal: The National Level*. Columbus: Ohio State University Press, 1975, p. 183.

4. John A. Salmond, "The Civilian Conservation Corps and the Negro," *Journal of American History* (1965), quoted in Braeman et al., *The New Deal*, p. 192. For a detailed analysis of the CCC's implementation, accomplishments, and effectiveness, see Salmond's *The Civilian Conservation Corps, 1933–1942: A New Deal Case Study*. Durham, NC: Duke University Press, 1967.

5. John P. Davis, "A Black Inventory of the New Deal," *The Crisis* (1935), quoted in William Dudley, ed., *The Great Depression: Opposing Viewpoints*. San Diego: Greenhaven Press, 1994, p. 188.

6. Davis, "A Black Inventory of the New Deal," in Dudley, *The Great Depression*, p. 189.

CHAPTER 3

Historical Assessment of the Great Depression and the New Deal

"There were ten million people unemployed all the time during the New Deal. That history has not been brought out clearly. Most of your historians of that period were New Dealers on the [government] payroll. . . . Everything pro–New Deal was written and almost nothing against it."

The New Deal Achieved Little

More than sixty years have passed since Franklin D. Roosevelt's administration imposed its New Deal agenda on the American people. In these decades the United States rose from the depths of the Great Depression, won World War II, and became the world's economic leader, as well as its great military superpower. Virtually none of this enormous success story can be attributed to the New Deal. In fact, by the eve of World War II in 1939, with the New Deal programs having been in place for over six years, the country was, overall, in little better shape than when Roosevelt first took office in 1933; and it was the nation's eventual entry into the European conflict, creating a gigantic surge of war production, that stimulated the economy and ended the Depression. "When the reform energies of the New Deal began to wane around 1939," says popular historian Howard Zinn,

> the nation was back to its normal state: a permanent army of unemployed; twenty or thirty million poverty-ridden people effectively blocked from

public view by a huge, prosperous, and fervently consuming middle class. . . . What the New Deal did was to refurbish middle-class America, which had taken a dizzying fall in the Depression, to restore jobs to half the jobless, and to give just enough to the lowest classes . . . to create an aura of good will.[1]

"Roosevelt didn't follow any particular policy after 1936," adds Raymond Moley, originally one of the president's closest advisors and later one of his staunchest critics.

Our economy began to slide downhill—our unemployment increased—after that, until 1940. This is something that liberals are not willing to recognize. It was the war that saved the economy and saved Roosevelt. . . . I think if it weren't for the war, Roosevelt probably would have been defeated in 1940.[2]

The early impression that it had been the New Deal, and not the war, that had saved the country came partly from the fact that the New Deal's failures and shortcomings were not often truthfully documented during the 1930s and early 1940s. "There were ten million people unemployed all the time during the New Deal," states Hamilton Fish, a Republican congressman and leading Roosevelt opponent during the Depression and war years.

That history has not been brought out clearly. Most of your historians of that period were New Dealers on the [government] payroll. He [Roosevelt] had a hundred million dollars to spend without making an account. He gave large sums of money to his friends, who were authors and writers. Everything pro–New Deal was written and almost nothing against it.[3]

Raymond Moley was one of those who managed to get his voice heard above the roar of the New Deal lackeys and apologists, although by the time people began to listen to him, it was too late; much in the way of time and resources had already been wasted. Shortly before the United States entered the war, he assessed the New Deal, saying that it had made a few minor gains. "But it is difficult to reconcile them with what they have cost," he wrote.

> It is not alone that . . . investment remains dormant, enterprise is chilled, the farmers' problem has not yet been solved, unemployment is colossal. It is that thousands of devoted men and women, who felt, as sincerely as Roosevelt, that we must redefine the aims of democratic government in terms of modern needs, have been alienated. . . . Their enthusiasm and their energies have been lost. . . . Extravagant promises have raised expectations far beyond any reasonable hope of realization.[4]

Popular journalist and social commentator H.L. Mencken was another boisterous critic of the New Deal in its heyday. He had the gall and courage to label Roosevelt a "quack doctor" who had "carried on his job with an ingratiating grin upon his face, like that of a snake-oil vendor at a village carnival," and who had shown no more sense of honor and morals than such a character. Harold Ickes, Frances Perkins, and the other leading New Dealers were "impudent nobodies," Mencken maintained, and their reign a "dreadful burlesque of civilized government."[5]

Mencken was thoroughly disillusioned with Roosevelt's policies, but he made the mistake of thinking that most of the American people agreed and that the Democrats would go down to defeat in 1936. They did not, of course; and it is reasonable to ask why the president and his cronies were so consistently successful at convincing the masses that the New Deal was in fact a *good* deal. The answer comes from noted French journalist Amaury de Riencourt, who from his foreign vantage offers a cool and unbiased observation of American politics and behavior:

What Roosevelt had to a supreme degree, was a charismatic charm that poured out naturally, the irresistible charm of a born leader of men. As soon as he was in office he communicated with the American people through his "fireside chats," a remarkable exercise in mass hypnotism. . . . A new device, the radio, had prevailed over the older printed word; and when his magnetic voice purred its way into the ears of millions of his compatriots, he managed to cast an unbreakable spell on America. . . . At this game, Franklin Roosevelt was unrivaled.[6]

Whatever the reasons for Roosevelt's popularity and success at keeping himself in power, Moley, Mencken, and other administration critics were vindicated later when, looking back from the convenient perspective of later decades, it

President Roosevelt speaks to the American public during one of his famous "fireside chats." Critics argue that the president lulled the nation into a false sense of security through his reassuring addresses.

became clear that the New Dealers had led the nation down the proverbial garden path. While listening to the president's reassurances on the radio, most Americans were blissfully unaware of the amount of power he had gradually amassed. This power was not only centralized in his staff and in the agencies he created, but especially, and ominously, in his own person; no American president before him, with the possible exception of Lincoln in the Civil War emergency, had ever wielded so much unbridled personal authority over the Congress, business and social institutions, and the lives of everyday people. In a very real sense, Roosevelt induced the American people, unknowingly of course, to trade many of their freedoms for a feeling of security, unfortunately one that turned out to be false. As de Riencourt puts it,

> Throughout the first year of his rule, Roosevelt concentrated on increasing the amount of power in his hands, overriding the reluctance of a disgruntled Congress. Administrative agencies assumed a degree of power and independence that left the legislative branch with very little influence on the dizzying course of events. . . . The spirit of the Roman *panem et circenses* [bread and circuses, that is, controlling the masses by appeasing them with free handouts] was slowly pervading the atmosphere, without destroying the willingness to work but weakening the former self-reliance of pioneering days. The mainstay of American freedom—freedom *from* authority—began to give way now that a large majority of the people were willing to barter freedom for security. . . . Under Franklin Roosevelt's New Deal, America took a decisive step toward Caesarism [the rule of benevolent dictators like Julius Caesar]. The remarkable feature of this subtle evolution was that it could take place constitutionally, without any illegal move, simply by stretching the extremely pliable fabric of America's political institutions.[7]

Indeed, thanks to Roosevelt's vast expansion of federal power, the relationship between American institutions, the people, and the government was permanently altered; the government now routinely regulates, legislates, or otherwise intrudes on nearly every aspect of American life. That unfortunate state of affairs is the real legacy of the New Deal.

1. Howard Zinn, "Introduction," in Howard Zinn, ed., *New Deal Thought*. Indianapolis: Bobbs-Merrill Company, 1966, p. xvi.

2. Quoted in Studs Terkel, *Hard Times: An Oral History of the Great Depression*. New York: Random House, 1970, pp. 251–52.

3. Quoted in Terkel, *Hard Times*, p. 291.

4. Raymond Moley, *After Seven Years*. New York: Harper and Brothers, 1939, pp. 399–400.

5. H.L. Mencken, "Three Years of Dr. Roosevelt," *The American Mercury* (1936), quoted in William E. Leuchtenburg, ed., *The New Deal: A Documentary History*. New York: Harper and Row, 1968, p. 201.

6. Amaury de Riencourt, "Caesarism Comes to America," in Morton Keller, ed., *The New Deal: What Was It?* New York: Holt, Rinehart and Winston, 1963, p. 107.

7. de Riencourt, "Caesarism," in Keller, *The New Deal*, p. 108.

"The shortcomings of the New Deal vanish in the general perspective of its supreme success: that is, in the restoration of . . . democracy as a workable way of life. . . . The New Deal took a broken and despairing land and gave it new confidence in itself."

The New Deal Was a Tremendous Achievement

The New Deal was far from perfect, for it was essentially a gigantic experiment in national economic and social theory; and in any experiment, one must expect some mistakes and failures due to trial and error. Yet the gamble President Roosevelt and his New Dealers took in shifting the country in a brave new direction paid off. In retrospect, the New Deal, when viewed as a whole, was a political, economic, and social achievement of epic proportions. A large portion of this achievement was material in nature. As noted historian Richard Hofstadter points out, it created

> a number of measures to make life more comfortable and secure, measures that would benefit not only contemporaries, but also millions of Americans yet to be born. After 1936, not even the Republicans quarreled in their party platforms with such reforms as the Social Security Act, minimum wages and hours, improved housing conditions for low-income families, or the insuring of bank deposits.[1]

It is an undisputed fact that before the New Deal, many of the government and social institutions and programs that Americans now take for granted, and indeed consider vital to their security and happiness, did not exist. There was no national old-age pension plan, no aid to dependent children, no federal housing, no federal compensation for the unemployed, no regulation of the stock market, no federal school lunch program for poor children, no minimum wages, and no government welfare system.

Many people today regard the last of these—welfare—as money badly spent, partly, they say, because it destroys the work ethic and also because many on the welfare rolls abuse the system. Yet even that system's staunchest critics admit that some minimum level of welfare is needed in a humane society; and this minimum level, and nothing more, is what the New Deal originally provided at a time when society's truly needy had quite literally nowhere else to turn. "The Depression had exhausted private, local, and state resources for relief before 1933," historian Anthony Badger explains.

> New Deal welfare programs gave the unemployed money and jobs. The lasting loyalty of low-income voters to Roosevelt expressed their appreciation of the very real and essential benefits they received. The Social Security Act created insurance for the old and unemployed which had existed nowhere in the public sector before and only minimally in the private sector. The Act initiated a quantum leap in the provision of assistance to the old, the blind, and dependent children. . . . The New Deal welfare programs provided direct assistance to perhaps as many as 35 percent of the population. It bequeathed a commitment to a minimum level of social welfare from which successive governments have never been entirely able to escape.[2]

The tally of other New Deal achievements that have made American life more comfortable and secure is enormous. In the economic realm, the 1933 Securities Act made company heads criminally liable for misinformation in their financial statements; and the 1934 Securities and Exchange Act provided for government supervision of the stock exchanges, making another crash like the one that initiated the Depression less likely. In housing, the 1933 Home Owners Loan Corporation refinanced home mortgages, saving tens of thousands from foreclosure; in 1934 the Federal Housing Administration began insuring construction loans, making it possible for millions of Americans to build or renovate their homes; and the 1935 Resettlement Administration erected whole new communities across the land and provided loans to desperate farmers and other rural Americans.[3] In addition, the New Deal wiped out most sweatshops, which exploited poor, desperate workers; removed over 150,000 child laborers from dangerous factory jobs; and improved working conditions in all workplaces by mandating minimum standards. Historian William Leuchtenburg, a noted authority on the New Deal, here lists just some of its other accomplishments:

> [It] recruited university-trained administrators, won control of the money supply, established central banking . . . fostered unionization of the factories . . . ended the tyranny of company towns . . . built camps for migrants, provided jobs for millions of unemployed . . . covered the American landscape with new edifices, subsidized painters and novelists, composers and ballet dancers, founded America's first state theater . . . generated electrical power [through the TVA and other such projects] . . . initiated the Soil Conservation Service . . . gave women greater recognition, [and] made a start toward breaking the pattern of racial discrimination and segregation.[4]

In addition to providing so many important and lasting material benefits for the nation, the New Deal greatly boosted the American people's morale at a time when it had reached a dangerously low ebb; and thereby it restored the country's belief in

*In addition to boosting the national economy, the New Deal also improved work-
ing conditions for American laborers by eliminating sweatshops and revising child
labor laws.*

itself and what it could achieve. "The New Deal had taken up a
people brought to the brink of despair by poverty and failure,"
remarks Hofstadter, "and had restored their morale. . . . The
New Deal restored their belief that a democratic people could
cope with its own problems in a democratic way."[5] Highly
respected historian Arthur M. Schlesinger agrees, stating:

> The great achievement of the New Deal was to intro-
> duce the United States to the twentieth century.
> Roosevelt redressed the defects of the Jeffersonian
> tradition by equipping the liberal party with a philos-
> ophy of government intervention— a belief, as he put
> it, that "the government has the definite duty to use
> all its power and resources to meet the new social
> problems with new social controls." Much of the
> New Deal was imperfect, abortive, or ambiguous. . . .
> But the shortcomings of the New Deal vanish in the
> general perspective of its supreme success: that is, in
> the restoration of America as a fighting faith, and in
> the restoration of democracy as a workable way of

life. . . . The New Deal took a broken and despairing land and gave it new confidence in itself.[6]

That new American confidence was fueled by an indomitable spirit flowing to the people directly from the New Deal's chief architect himself. In the final analysis, what made the New Deal work and laid the foundations for a better country was the courageous, tireless, and inspiring leadership of one special man who refused to be beaten by a crippling disability; a heroic personal victory over pain and fear was translated into a nation's resurgent belief in its own abilities and destiny. Schlesinger points out:

> The essence of Roosevelt, the quality which fulfilled the best in him . . . was his intrepid and passionate affirmation. He always cast his vote for life, for action, for forward motion, for the future. . . . He responded to what was vital, not to what was lifeless; to what was coming, not to what was passing away. He lived by his exultation in distant horizons and uncharted seas. It was this that won him confidence and loyalty in a frightened age . . . and the conviction of plain people that he had given them head and heart and would not cease fighting in their cause.[7]

1. Richard Hofstadter et al., *The United States: The History of a Republic.* Englewood Cliffs, NJ: Prentice-Hall, 1957, pp. 674–75.

2. Anthony J. Badger, *The New Deal: The Depression Years, 1933–1940.* New York: Farrar, Straus and Giroux, 1989, p. 301.

3. These farmers' loans began in 1937 when the Resettlement Administration was reorganized as the Farm Security Administration (FSA). By June 1944 the FSA had given financial assistance to over 870,000 needy rural families.

4. William Leuchtenburg, "The Achievement of the New Deal," in William Dudley, ed., *The Great Depression: Opposing Viewpoints.* San Diego: Greenhaven Press, 1994, pp. 277–78.

5. Hofstadter et al., *The United States,* pp. 674–75.

6. Arthur M. Schlesinger Jr., "The Broad Accomplishments of the New Deal," in Edwin C. Rozwenc, ed., *The New Deal: Revolution or Evolution?* Boston: D.C. Heath, 1949, p. 101.

7. Arthur M. Schlesinger Jr., *The Coming of the New Deal.* Boston: Houghton Mifflin, 1959, p. 588.

APPENDIX A

Excerpts from Original Documents Pertaining to the Great Depression and the New Deal

Document 1: Herbert Hoover Opposes Big Government

In October 1928, near the close of the presidential election campaign, Republican candidate Herbert Hoover delivered his now famous "rugged individualism" speech, excerpted here, in which he touted the "American system" of self-reliance and decried the evils of an intrusive, overcontrolling government.

During 150 years we have builded up a form of self-government and a social system which is peculiarly our own. It differs essentially from all others in the world. It is the American system. It is just as definite and positive a political and social system as has ever been developed on earth. It is founded upon a particular conception of self-government in which decentralized local responsibility is the very base. Further than this, it is founded upon the conception that only through ordered liberty, freedom and equal opportunity to the individual will his initiative and enterprise spur on the march of progress. And in our insistence upon equality of opportunity has our system advanced beyond all the world.

During the war we necessarily turned to the Government to solve every difficult economic problem. The Government having absorbed every energy of our people for war, there was no other solution. For the preservation of the State the Federal Government became a centralized despotism which undertook unprecedented responsibilities, assumed autocratic powers, and took over the business of citizens. To a large degree we regimented our whole people temporarily into a socialistic state. However justified in time of war if continued in peace time it would destroy not only our American system but with it our progress and freedom as well.

When the war closed, the most vital of all issues both in our own country and throughout the world was whether Governments should continue their wartime ownership and operation of many instrumentalities of production and distribution. We were challenged with a peace-time choice between the American system of rugged individualism and a European philosophy of diametrically opposed doctrines—doctrines of paternalism and state socialism. The acceptance of these ideas would have meant the destruction of self-government through centralization of government. It would have meant the undermining of the individual initiative and enterprise through which our people have grown to unparalleled greatness.

The Republican Party from the beginning resolutely turned its face away from these ideas and these war practices. . . . When the Republican Party came into full power it went at once resolutely back to our fundamental conception of the State and the rights and responsibilities of the individual. . . .

There has been revived in this campaign, however, a series of proposals which, if adopted, would be a long step toward the abandonment of our American system and a surrender to the destructive operation of governmental conduct of commercial business. . . .

There is, therefore, submitted to the American people a question of fundamental principle. That is: shall we depart from the principles of our American political and economic system, upon which we have advanced beyond all the rest of the world, in order to adopt methods based on principles destructive of its very foundations? And I wish to emphasize the seriousness of these proposals. I wish to make my position clear; for this goes to the very roots of American life and progress.

I should like to state to you the effect that this projection of government in business would have upon our system of self-government and our economic system. That effect would reach to the daily life of every man and woman. It would impair the very basis of liberty and freedom not only for those left outside the fold of expanded bureaucracy but for those embraced within it.

Let us first see the effect upon self-government. When the Federal Government undertakes to go into commercial business it must at once set up the organization and administration of that business, and it immediately finds itself in a labyrinth, every alley of which leads to the destruction of self-government.

Commercial business requires a concentration of responsibility. Self-government requires decentralization and many checks and balances to safeguard liberty. Our Government to succeed in business would need become in effect a despotism. There at once begins the destruction of self-government. . . .

It is a false liberalism that interprets itself into the Government operation of commercial business. Every step of bureaucratizing of the business of our country poisons the very roots of liberalism—that is, political equality, free speech, free assembly, free press, and equality of opportunity. It is the road not to more liberty, but to less liberty. Liberalism should be found not striving to spread bureaucracy but striving to set bounds to it. True liberalism seeks all legitimate freedom, first in the confident belief that without such freedom the pursuit of all other blessings and benefits is vain. That belief is the foundation of all American progress, political as well as economic. . . .

Our people have the right to know whether we can continue to solve our great problems without abandonment of our American system. I know we can. . . .

And what have been the results of our American system? Our country has become the land of opportunity to those born without inheritance, not merely because of the wealth of its resources and industry, but because of this freedom of initiative and enterprise. . . .

By adherence to the principles of decentralized self-government, ordered liberty, equal opportunity and freedom to the individual, our American experiment in human welfare has yielded a degree of well-being unparalleled in all the world. It has come nearer to the abolition of poverty, to the abolition of fear of want, than humanity has ever reached before. Progress of the past seven years is the proof of it. This alone furnishes the answer to our opponents who ask us to introduce destructive elements into the system by which this has been accomplished. . . .

I have endeavored to present to you that the greatness of America has grown out of a political and social system and a method of control of economic forces distinctly its own—our American system—which has carried this great experiment in human welfare further than ever before in all history. We are nearer today to the ideal of the abolition of poverty and fear from the lives of men and women than ever before in any land. And I again repeat that the departure from our American system by injecting principles destructive to it which our opponents propose will jeopardize the very liberty and freedom of our people, will destroy equality of opportunity, not alone to ourselves but to our children.

Richard Hofstadter, ed., *Great Issues in American History: A Documentary Record, Volume II, 1864–1957*. New York: Vintage Books, 1960, pp. 338–43.

Document 2: Black "Progress" Before the New Deal

Following is an excerpt from a speech delivered by President Hoover on April 14, 1931, in which he praised the strides that black Americans had supposedly made in education and other areas since gaining their freedom. The long and difficult struggle for educational, economic, and social equality that blacks underwent in the decades that followed demonstrated that they had in reality made little progress before the New Deal and that Hoover's words were mostly empty rhetoric.

It is now over sixty years since the Negro was released from slavery and given the status of a citizen in our country, whose wealth and general prosperity his labor has helped create. The progress of the race within this period has surpassed the most sanguine hopes of the most ardent advocates. No group of people in history ever started from a more complete economic and cultural destitution. . . .

The greatest single factor in the progress of the Negro race has been the schools, private and public, established and conducted by high-minded, self-sacrificing men and women of both races and all sections of the country, maintained by the States and by private philanthropy, covering the whole field of education from primary school through to college and university. These public and private schools particularly, under the leadership of Tuskegee and other universities and colleges, have been the most effective agents in solving the problems created by the admission to citizenship of 4,000,000 ex-slaves without preparation for their new responsibilities. That such a revolution in the social order did not produce a more serious upheaval in our national existence has been due to the constructive influence exerted by these educational institutions, whose maintenance of further development is both a public and private duty.

The nation owes a debt of gratitude to the wisdom and constructive vision of Booker T. Washington, the founder of Tuskegee. His conception of education, based fundamentally upon vocational and moral training, has been worthily continued by his able successor, Dr. R.R. Moton, who likewise deserves the gratitude of the nation for his many contributions to the solution of one of our most difficult national problems. His ability and sanity and modesty have been powerful forces in progress and good will.

"Address of April 14, 1931, commemorating the anniversary of the founding of Tuskegee Institute," quoted in William S. Myers and Walter H. Newton, *The Hoover Administration: A Documented Narrative*. New York: Charles Scribner's Sons, 1936, pp. 474–75.

Document 3: A Spectacle of National Degeneration

In May 1932, with unemployment, hunger, and other ravages of the Depression steadily worsening, Joseph L. Heffernan, mayor of Youngstown, Ohio, penned this tract, which is both a lament on the failure of relief efforts and a warning about the potential long-term harm posed to American self-esteem by the need to resort to taking charity.

Often, as I have watched the line of job seekers at the City Hall, I have had occasion to marvel at the mysterious power that certain words and phrases exercise upon the human mind. A wise man once observed that words rule mankind, and so it is in America today. Prominent politicians and business men have repeatedly stated that, come what may, America must not have the dole. To be sure, we should all be much happier if we could get along without a dole, but the simple truth is that we have it already. Every city in the land has had a dole from the moment it began unemployment relief. The men who apply for help know that it is a dole. The officials who issue work orders can be in no doubt about it, for the work done in no way justifies the money spent, except on the basis of a dole.

Why, then, so much concern about the word? Perhaps because, if we were honest enough to recognize unemployment relief for the dole it really is, we should also have to be honest enough to admit that the depression is a catastrophe of historic proportions, and courageous enough to deal with it accordingly. One alternative to the dole would be to let all the unfortunates starve to death, but so far no one has advanced this proposal, although some have come pretty close to it in saying that the way out of the depression is to let nature take its course.

Those who have not been willing to go so far as that have maintained, however, that each community must look after its own unemployed, and that under no circumstances must the Federal Government assume any responsibility for them. For two years local communities have carried the burden unassisted, and many of them, like Youngstown, have prostrated themselves in doing it. We of the cities have done our best, laboring against conditions which were beyond our control. But, even if we are given full credit for trying, we must now admit that we have failed miserably. Whether this was caused by a lack of simple charity in the hearts of our people or by our incapacity to manage our financial problems is beside the point. The fact of our failure is patent. We of the cities have not advanced a single new idea on unemployment or its relief. We have not dared to consider the fundamental questions raised by our social and economic collapse. We are still as stupidly devoted as ever to the philosophy of *laissez faire*, and we face the future bewildered and purposeless. Our one great achievement in response to this national catastrophe has been to open soup kitchens and flop-houses.

And nobody has taken the trouble to weigh the consequences of our well-meant but ineffective charity upon the moral fibre of the American people. Seventy years ago we fought a civil war to free black slaves; to-day we remain indifferent while millions of our fellow citizens are reduced to the status of paupers. There is a world of difference between mere poverty and pauperism. The honest poor will struggle for years to keep themselves above the pauper class. With quiet desperation they will bear hunger and mental anguish until every resource is exhausted. Then comes the ultimate struggle when, with heartache and an overwhelming sense of disgrace, they have to make the shamefaced journey to the door of public charity. This is the last straw. Their self-respect is destroyed; they undergo an insidious metamorphosis, and sink down to spiritless despondency.

This descent from respectability, frequent enough in the best of times, has been hastened immeasurably by two years of business paralysis, and the people who have been affected in this manner must be numbered in millions. This is what we have accomplished with our bread lines and soup kitchens. I know, because I have seen thousands of these defeated, discouraged, hopeless men and women, cringing and fawning as they come to ask for public aid. It is a spectacle of national degeneration. That is the fundamental tragedy for America. If every mill and factory in the land should begin to hum with prosperity to-morrow morning, the destructive effect of our haphazard relief measures would not work itself out of the nation's blood until the sons of our sons have expiated the sins of our neglect.

Joseph L. Heffernan, "The Hungry City: A Mayor's Experience with Unemployment," *Atlantic Monthly*, May 1932.

Document 4: Roosevelt Promises Americans a New Deal

In accepting the Democratic Party's nomination for the presidency on July 2, 1932, Franklin D. Roosevelt, then governor of New York State, promised the American people that the policies of the past were about to end and that a better future was about to begin. In the conclusion of the speech, he coined the term "New Deal," which would ever after be synonymous with his presidency.

At last our eyes are open. At last the American people are ready to acknowledge that Republican leadership was wrong and that the Democracy is right.

My program, of which I can only touch on these points, is based upon this simple moral principle: the welfare and the soundness of a Nation depend first upon what the great mass of the people wish and need; and second, whether or not they are getting it.

What do the people of America want more than anything else? To my mind, they want two things: work, with all the moral and spiritual values that go with it; and with work, a reasonable measure of security—security for themselves and for their wives and children. Work and security—these are more than words. They are more than facts. They are the spiritual values, the true goal toward which our efforts of reconstruction should lead. These are the values that this program is intended to gain; these are the values we have failed to achieve by the leadership we now have.

Our Republican leaders tell us economic laws—sacred, inviolable, unchangeable—cause panics which no one could prevent. But while they prate of economic laws, men and women are starving. We must lay hold of the fact that economic laws are not made by nature. They are made by human beings. . . .

I say that while primary responsibility for relief rests with localities now, as ever, yet the Federal Government has always had and still has a continuing responsibility for the broader public welfare. It will soon fulfill that responsibility. . . .

Never before in modern history have the essential differences between the two major American parties stood out in such striking contrast as they do today. Republican leaders not only have failed in material things, they have failed in national vision, because in disaster they have held out no hope, they have pointed out no path for the people below to climb back to places of security and of safety in our American life.

Throughout the Nation, men and women, forgotten in the political philosophy of the Government of the last years look to us here for guidance and for more equitable opportunity to share in the distribution of national wealth.

On the farms, in the large metropolitan areas, in the smaller cities and in the villages, millions of our citizens cherish the hope that their old standards of living and of thought have not gone forever. Those millions cannot and shall not hope in vain.

I pledge you, I pledge myself, to a new deal for the American people. Let us all here assembled constitute ourselves prophets of a new order of competence and of courage. This is more than a political campaign; it is a call to arms. Give me your help, not to win votes alone, but to win in this crusade to restore America to its own people.

Samuel I. Rosenman, ed., *The Public Papers and Addresses of Franklin D. Roosevelt*. Vol. I. New York: Russell and Russell, 1969, pp. 657–59.

Document 5: Roosevelt Declares War on the Depression

Following are excerpts from Franklin D. Roosevelt's first inaugural address, delivered on March 4, 1933, in which he galvanized the nation with a stirring call to "wage a war" against the economic and social crisis the nation then faced.

This is a day of national consecration, and I am certain that my fellow-Americans expect that on my induction into the Presidency I will address them with a candor and a decision which the present situation of our nation impels.

This is pre-eminently the time to speak the truth, the whole truth, frankly and boldly. Nor need we shrink from honestly facing conditions in our country today. This great nation will endure as it has endured, will revive and will prosper.

So first of all let me assert my firm belief that the only thing we have to fear is fear itself—nameless, unreasoning, unjustified terror which paralyzes needed efforts to convert retreat into advance.

In every dark hour of our national life a leadership of frankness and vigor has met with that understanding and support of the people themselves which is essential to victory. I am convinced that you will again give that support to leadership in these critical days. . . .

Our greatest primary task is to put people to work. This is no unsolvable problem if we face it wisely and courageously.

It can be accomplished in part by direct recruiting by the government itself, treating the task as we would treat the emergency of a war, but at the same time, through this employment, accomplishing greatly needed projects to stimulate and reorganize the use of our natural resources.

Hand in hand with this, we must frankly recognize the overbalance of population in our industrial centers and, by engaging on a national scale in a redistribution, endeavor to provide a better use of the land for those best fitted for the land. . . .

If I read the temper of our people correctly, we now realize as we have never realized before, our interdependence on each other; that we cannot merely take, but we must give as well; that if we are to go forward we must move as a trained and loyal army willing to sacrifice for the good of a common discipline, because, without such discipline, no progress is made, no leadership becomes effective.

We are, I know, ready and willing to submit our lives and property to such discipline because it makes possible a leadership which aims at a larger good.

This I propose to offer, pledging that the larger purposes will bind upon us all as a sacred obligation with a unity of duty hitherto evoked only in time of armed strife.

With this pledge taken, I assume unhesitatingly the leadership of this great army of our people, dedicated to a disciplined attack upon our common problems. . . .

It is to be hoped that the normal balance of executive and legislative authority may be wholly adequate to meet the unprecedented task before us. But it may be that an unprecedented demand and need for undelayed action may call for temporary departure from that normal balance of public procedure.

I am prepared under my constitutional duty to recommend the measures that a stricken nation in the midst of a stricken world may require.

These measures, or such other measures as the Congress may build out of its experience and wisdom, I shall seek, within my constitutional authority, to bring to speedy adoption. . . .

I shall ask the Congress for the one remaining instrument to meet the crisis—broad executive power to wage a war against the emergency as great as the power that would be given to me if we were in fact invaded by a foreign foe.

For the trust reposed in me I will return the courage and the devotion that befit the time. I can do no less.

We face the arduous days that lie before us in the warm courage of national unity; with the clear consciousness of seeking old and precious moral values; with the clean satisfaction that comes from the stern performance of duty by old and young alike. . . .

In this dedication of a nation we humbly ask the blessing of God. May He protect each and every one of us! May He guide me in the days to come!

Richard Hofstadter, ed., *Great Issues in American History: A Documentary Record, Volume II, 1864–1957.* New York: Vintage Books, 1960, pp. 352–57.

Document 6: Huey Long Calls for Sharing the Wealth

In 1935 Senator Huey P. Long of Louisiana presented to Congress his proposal for a national economic redistribution plan, asserting that the United States could overcome the ravages of the Depression if it adopted the following measures.

Here is the whole sum and substance of the Share Our Wealth movement:

1. Every family to be furnished by the Government a homestead allowance, free of debt, of not less than one-third the average family wealth of the country, which means, at the lowest, that every family shall have the reasonable comforts of life up to a value of from $5,000 to $6,000. No person to have a fortune of more than 100 to 300 times the average family fortune, which means that the limit to fortunes is between $1,500,000 and $5,000,000, with annual capital levy taxes imposed on all above $1,000,000.

2. The yearly income of every family shall not be less than one-third of the average family income, which means that, according to the estimates of the statisticians of the United States Government and Wall Street, no family's annual income would be less than from $2,000 to $2,500. No yearly income shall be allowed to any person larger than from 100 to 300 times the size of the average family income, which means that no person would be allowed to earn in any year more than from $600,000 to $1,800,000, all to be subject to present income-tax laws.

3. To limit or regulate the hours of work to such an extent as to prevent overproduction; the most modern and efficient machinery would be encouraged, so that as much would be produced as possible so as to satisfy all demands of the people, but to also allow the maximum time to the workers for recreation, convenience, education, and luxuries of life.

4. An old age pension to the persons over 60.

5. To balance agricultural production with what can be consumed according to the laws of God, which includes the preserving and storage of surplus commodities to be paid for and held by the Government for the emergencies when such are needed. Please bear in mind, however, that when the people of America have had money to buy things they needed, we have never had a surplus of any commodity. This plan of God does not call for destroying any of the things raised to eat or wear, nor does it countenance wholesale destruction of hogs, cattle, or milk.

6. To pay the veterans of our wars what we owe them and to care for their disabled.

7. Education and training for all children to be equal in opportunity in all schools, colleges, universities, and other institutions for training in the professions and vocations of life; to be regulated on the capacity of children to learn, and not upon the ability of parents to pay the costs. Training for life's work to be as much universal and thorough for all walks in life as has been the training in the arts of killing.

8. The raising of revenue and taxes for the support of this program to come from the reduction of swollen fortunes from the top, as well as for the support of public works to give employment whenever there may be any slackening necessary in private enterprise.

I now ask those who read this circular to help us at once in this work of giving life and happiness to our people—not a starvation dole upon which someone may live in misery from week to week. Before this miserable system of wreckage has destroyed the life germ of respect and culture in our American people let us save what was here, merely by having none too poor and none too rich. The theory of the Share Our Wealth Society is to have enough for all, but not to have one with so much that less than enough remains for the balance of the people.

Letter published in *Congressional Record*, 74th Congress, 2nd Session, vol. 79, no. 107, May 23, 1935: 8, 333–36.

Document 7: Social Security Offers a "Measure of Protection"

At the historic signing ceremony of the 1935 Social Security Act, President Roosevelt thanked Congress for helping give the American people a "patriotic" piece of legislation.

Today a hope of many years' standing is in large part fulfilled. The civilization of the past hundred years, with its startling industrial changes, has tended more and more to make life insecure. Young people have come to wonder what would be their lot when they came to old age. The man with a job has wondered how long the job would last.

This social security measure gives at least some protection to thirty millions of our citizens who will reap direct benefits through unemployment compensation, through old-age pensions and through increased services for the protection of children and the prevention of ill health.

We can never insure one hundred percent of the population against one hundred percent of the hazards and vicissitudes of life, but we have tried to frame a law which will give some measure of protection to the average citizen and to his family against the loss of a job and against poverty-ridden old age.

This law, too, represents a cornerstone in a structure which is being built but is by no means complete. It is a structure intended to lessen the force of possible future depressions. It will act as a protection to future Administrations against the necessity of going deeply into debt to furnish relief to the needy. The law will flatten out the peaks and valleys of deflation and of inflation. It is, in short, a law that will take care of human needs and at the same time provide for the United States an economic structure of vastly greater soundness.

I congratulate all of you ladies and gentlemen, all of you in the Congress, in the executive departments and all of you who come from private life, and I thank you for your splendid efforts in behalf of this sound, needed and patriotic legislation.

If the Senate and the House of Representatives in this long and arduous session had done nothing more than pass this Bill, the session would be regarded as historic for all time.

"Presidential Statement upon Signing the Social Security Act, August 14, 1935," in Samuel I. Rosenman, ed., *The Public Papers and Addresses of Franklin D. Roosevelt*, Vol. 4. New York: Russell and Russell, 1969, pp. 324–25.

Document 8: The President Seduced by Power?

In this excerpt from his book After Seven Years, *former Roosevelt adviser Raymond Moley, who became one of the New Deal's chief critics, accuses the president of succumbing to the age-old bane of rulers—the corruptive effects of holding and wielding great power.*

The one factor [of Franklin Roosevelt's character] of which I never dreamed was the intensifying and exhilarating effect of power upon such a temperament.

For Roosevelt in 1932 was not immodest. He listened patiently to advice. No one respected more than he the right of others to their own opinions. No one seemed less likely to be overwhelmed by the illusion of his own rectitude. He was the batter who had no expectation of making a hit every time he came up to bat. . . .

I would not have believed that Roosevelt would succumb to the unlovely habits of "telling, not asking," of brusquely brushing aside well-meant tenders of information and advice. . . .

I could not imagine that the quality of refusing to admit defeat would become the incapacity to admit error except in the vaguest of generalities.

I could not imagine Roosevelt's envisaging himself as the beneficiary of a vote based upon the challenge that he was the issue, that people must either be friends of the friendless, and hence "for him," or enemies of the friendless, and hence "against him."

I could not imagine that a growing identification of self with the will of the people would lead him on to an attempted impairment of those very institutions and methods which have made progressive evolution possible in this country.

But then, I did not reckon with what seemed, in a United States which cried out for action and assertion, perhaps the most irrelevant political axiom wise men through the ages had ever devised. I had not yet learned that no temperament, however fluid, is immune to the vitrifying effect of power. . . .

Power itself has ways of closing the windows of a President's mind to fresh, invigorating currents of opinion from the outside. The most important of these ways is the subtle flattery with which the succession of those who see the President day after day treat him. Nine out of ten of those who see a President want something of him, and, because they do, they are likely to tell him something pleasant, something to cozen his good will. They are likely to agree with him, rather than disagree with him. If a man is told he is right by people day after day, he will, unless he has extraordinary defenses, ultimately believe he can never be wrong.

Until the very end of my association with Roosevelt, I hoped that his quality of pragmatism would keep some of the windows of his mind open. I finally found that he was not only being shut in by the usual process of flattery but that he himself was slamming shut windows. He developed a very special method of reassuring himself of his own preconceptions after hearing an unwelcome bit of advice. This consisted of telling Visitor B that he had just heard so-and-so from Visitor A and that A was "scared" about something, or that A didn't know what he was talking about. Usually B would agree with the President. But whether or not he did, if he was a man of spirit he decided that he, for one, wouldn't put himself into the position of being made ridiculous to Visitor C. So he would withhold all disagreement by way of self-protection. And so was another window closed.

Raymond Moley, *After Seven Years*. New York: Harper and Brothers, 1939, pp. 396–97.

Documents 9, 10, and 11: Depression Memories

Three people of very different walks of life here give their personal recollections of various aspects of the Depression years. In the first quote, Mary Owsley, who lived with her husband in Oklahoma from 1929 to 1936, remembers the terrible toll the crisis took on people in America's rural heartland; in the second, wealthy businessman Arthur A. Robertson, who did not suffer financially during the Depression, describes other rich individuals who did; the third quote is by George

Tallen, in his teens and early twenties during the Depression, who vividly recalls hard work, the repeal of Prohibition, and dealing with prejudice in the small Missouri town of Moberly.

There was thousands of people out of work in Oklahoma City. They set up a soup line, and the food was clean and it was delicious. Many, many people, colored and white, I didn't see any difference, 'cause there was just as many white people out of work than were colored. Lost everything they had accumulated from their young days. And these are facts. I remember several families had to leave in covered wagons. To Californy, I guess.

See, the oil boom come in '29. People come from every direction in there. A coupla years later, they was livin' in everything from pup tents, houses built out of cardboard boxes and old pieces of metal that they'd pick up—anything that they could find to put somethin' together to put a wall around 'em to protect 'em from the public.

I knew one family there in Oklahoma City, a man and a woman and seven children lived in a hole in the ground. You'd be surprised how nice it was, how nice they kept it. They had chairs and tables and beds back in that hole. And they had the dirt all braced up there, just like a cave.

Oh, the dust storms, they were terrible. You could wash and hang clothes on a line, and if you happened to be away from the house and couldn't get those clothes in before that storm got there, you'd never wash that out. Oil was in that sand. It'd color them the most awful color you ever saw. It just ruined them. They was just never fit to use, actually. I had to use 'em, understand, but they wasn't very presentable. Before my husband was laid off, we lived in a good home. It wasn't a brick house, but it wouldn't have made any difference. These storms, when they would hit, you had to clean house from the attic to ground. Everything was covered in sand. Red sand, just full of oil.

The majority of people were hit and hit hard. They were mentally disturbed you're bound to know, 'cause they didn't know when the end of all this was comin'. There was a lot of suicides that I know of. From nothin' else but just they couldn't see any hope for a better tomorrow. I absolutely know some who did. Part of 'em were farmers and part of 'em were businessmen, even. They went flat broke and they committed suicide on the strength of it, nothing else.

. . . . . .

In the early Thirties, I was known as a scavenger. I used to buy broken-down businesses that banks took over. That was one of my best eras of prosperity. The whole period was characterized by men who were legends. When you talked about $1 million you were talking about loose change. Three or four of these men would get together, run up a stock to ridiculous prices and unload it on the unsuspecting public. The minute you heard of a man like Durant or Jesse Livermore buying stock, everybody followed. They knew it was going to go up. The only problem was to get out before they dumped it.

Durant owned General Motors twice and lost it twice . . . was worth way in excess of a billion dollars on paper, by present standards, four or five billion. He started his own automobile company, and it went under. When the Crash came, he caved in, like the rest of 'em. The last I heard of him I was told he ended up running a bowling alley. It was all on paper. Everybody in those days expected the sun to shine forever.

October 29, 1929, yeah. A frenzy. I must have gotten calls from a dozen and a half friends who were desperate. In each case, there was no sense in loaning them the money that they would give the broker. Tomorrow they'd be worse off than yesterday. Suicides, left and right, made a terrific impression on me, of course. People I knew. It was heartbreaking. One day you saw the prices at a hundred, the next day at $20, at $15.

On Wall Street, the people walked around like zombies. It was like *Death Takes a Holiday*. It was very dark. You saw people who yesterday rode around in Cadillacs lucky now to have carfare.

One of my friends said to me, "If things keep on as they are, we'll all have to go begging." I asked, "Who from?"

. . . .

Poverty is relative. We lived in poverty only we didn't know it. We lived much lower than most people on welfare today. But there were people who lived lower than us. We were sort of lower middle class. But we all worked. . . . I guess my early memories [of the Depression] are of working all the time. There was never a time in my youth when I could sit in a chair in [my] living quarters except when we had company. At noon, I'd walk home from school (about a mile), stay in the store (we had a small retail counter with candy and ice cream) while my dad and mother ate lunch, then they'd take over, I'd eat lunch and walk back to school. . . . The second biggest happening of that period (after the bank holiday) was the repeal of the 18th Amendment [Prohibition]. . . . This had a big influence on people, jobs, development, and community. Up until this time, the only place people could visit [in a small town] would be the confectionery. How long could you sit there with a sundae? [Most] people didn't sit in restaurants because they couldn't afford to eat out. When they did, it was in little places that were so small that there was no room to sit and visit. Now when we had our beer taverns [after Prohibition's repeal], people had a place to go. For a dime you could get a 32 oz. schooner of beer and could sit all day and night and talk and visit with everybody. . . . Nowadays [there is a misconception] that the only people who suffered prejudice [during the Depression] were black people. . . . That isn't true. . . . Poor whites [also] suffered prejudice. In the '30s [in] most places only the Irish had been accepted. The exceptions were where you had big populations of a certain nationality. Like in St. Louis, there were Greek neighborhoods, Italian, German, and various others. In the cities . . . they all lived together in their own neighborhoods. . . . But in most of the country (small towns and farms which had most of the population) there were not these large concentrations [of ethnic groups]. In Moberly, I was called a goddamned Greek—people would lean out of the car window to tell me to go back where I came from. The same for other national groups, mostly from eastern and southern Europe. . . . Jews—they had a bad time. My father told me to pay no attention. He said, "Do your work, do good at school, behave yourself, and laugh when people . . . try to berate you.". . . Because I was able to get around the name-calling, I taught many other kids, mostly blacks, how to react [to prejudice] and [thereby] how to make their lives [a little] better.

Mary Owsley and Arthur Robertson, quoted in Studs Terkel, *Hard Times: An Oral History of the Great Depression.* New York: Random House, 1970, pp. 45–46 and 66–67; George Tallen, quoted from a previously unpublished 1997 interview with Don Nardo.

Document 12: What the New Deal Achieved

This generally positive assessment of the accomplishments of the New Deal was penned by respected historian William Leuchtenburg in the early 1980s in commemoration of the fiftieth anniversary of its launching by President Roosevelt.

The Great Depression and the New Deal brought about a significant political realignment of the sort that occurs only rarely in America. The Depression wrenched many lifelong Republican voters from their moorings. In 1928, one couple christened their newborn son "Herbert Hoover Jones." Four years later they petitioned the court, "desiring to relieve the young man from the chagrin and mortification which he is suffering and will suffer," and asked that his name be changed to Franklin D. Roosevelt Jones. In 1932 FDR became the first Democrat to enter the White House with as much as 50 percent of the popular vote in eighty years—since Franklin K. Pierce in 1852. Roosevelt took advantage of this opportunity to mold "the FDR coalition," an alliance centered in the low-income districts of the great cities and, as recently as the 1980 election, the contours of the New Deal coalition could still be discerned. . . .

Furthermore, the New Deal drastically altered the agenda of American politics. When Arthur Krock of the *New York Times* listed the main programmatic questions before the 1932 Democratic convention, he wrote: "What would be said about the repeal of prohibition that had split the Republicans? What would be said about tariffs?" By 1936, these concerns seemed altogether old fashioned, as campaigners discussed the Tennessee Valley Authority and industrial relations, slum clearance and aid to the jobless. That year, a Little Rock newspaper commented: "Such matters as tax and tariff laws have given way to universally human things, the living problems and opportunities of the average man and the average family.". . .

What then did the New Deal do? It gave far greater amplitude to the national state, expanded the authority of the presidency, recruited university-trained administrators, won control of the money supply, established central banking, imposed regulation on Wall Street, rescued the debt-ridden farmer and homeowner, built model communities, financed the Federal Housing Administration, made federal housing a permanent feature, fostered unionization of the factories, reduced child labor, ended the tyranny of company towns, wiped out many sweatshops, mandated minimal working standards, enabled tenants to buy their own farms, built camps for migrants, introduced the welfare state with old-age pensions, unemployment insurance, and aid for dependent children, provided jobs for millions of unemployed, created a special program for the jobless young and for students, covered the American landscape with new edifices, subsidized painters and novelists, composers and ballet dancers, founded America's first state theater, created documentary films, gave birth to the impressive Tennessee Valley Authority, generated electrical power, sent the Civilian Conservation Corps boys into the forests, initiated the Soil Conservation Service, transformed the economy of agriculture, lighted up rural America, gave women greater recognition, made a start toward breaking the pattern of racial discrimination and segregation, put together a liberal party coalition, changed the agenda of American politics, and brought about a Constitutional Revolution. . . .

By restoring to the debate over the significance of the New Deal acknowledgment of its achievements, we may hope to produce a more judicious estimate of where it succeeded and where it failed. For it unquestionably did fail in a number of respects. There were experiments of the 1930s which miscarried, opportunities that were fumbled, groups who were neglected, and power that was arrogantly used. Over the whole performance lies the dark cloud of the persistence of hard times. The shortcomings of the New Deal are formidable, and they must be recognized. But I am not persuaded that the New Deal experience was negligible. Indeed, it is hard to think of another period in the whole history of the republic that was so fruitful or of a crisis that was met with as much imagination.

William E. Leuchtenburg, "The Achievements of the New Deal," in William Dudley, ed., *The Great Depression: Opposing Viewpoints*. San Diego: Greenhaven Press, 1994, pp. 276–78.

CHRONOLOGY

October 1928
In New York during the national presidential campaign, Republican candidate Herbert Hoover delivers his "rugged individualism" speech, redefining the traditional American values of self-reliance and the federal government playing a minimal role in people's lives.

November 1928
Hoover is elected president, defeating his Democratic opponent, Alfred E. Smith, by a wide margin.

October 1929
The New York Stock Market crashes, sending the U.S. economy into a disastrous tailspin; in the following two years, the nation sinks into a severe economic depression; the rest of the industrialized world quickly follows suit.

December 1930
The once-powerful Bank of the United States, along with many other smaller banks, fails; 4.5 million Americans are now unemployed.

April 1931
As the Great Depression tightens its grip, automobile tycoon Henry Ford lays off 75,000 workers.

January 1932
President Hoover signs into law the Reconstruction Finance Corporation, designed to help put banks and large businesses back on their feet.

July 1932
Franklin D. Roosevelt, governor of New York State, gains the Democratic presidential nomination for the upcoming election.

September 1932
Roosevelt delivers his "Commonwealth Club" speech, in which he asserts that government owes every citizen a right to life and a measure of security and happiness.

November 1932
Roosevelt defeats Hoover in a landslide, winning the electoral vote by a margin of 472 to 59.

March 1933
U.S. unemployment reaches a devastating 15 million
inaugurated as the thirty-second president; in his stir
address, he tells his countrymen that "the only thing we have to fear
is fear itself"; the president shuts down U.S. banks and orders that
their books be examined; Roosevelt gives his first radio "fireside
chat"; the president submits to Congress the Agricultural
Adjustment Act and the Civilian Conservation Corps, launching the
massive legislative assault on the Depression known thereafter as
the New Deal.

May 1933
Congress passes the Federal Emergency Relief Act, Emergency
Farm Mortgage Act, Truth in Securities Act, and the Tennessee
Valley Authority Act, the last of these designed to reshape the water
system of the Tennessee River Valley and to provide cheap electric-
ity for millions of Americans.

June 1933
Congress passes Roosevelt's National Industrial Recovery Act and
Home Owners Loan Act.

December 1933
The Eighteenth Amendment to the Constitution, prohibiting the
sale of alcoholic beverages, is repealed.

June 1934
Roosevelt signs into law the Securities Exchange Act, which initiates federal regulation of trading practices.

July 1934
The Federal Communications Commission (FCC) is created, providing for federal regulation of radio, telegraph, and cable businesses; Congress passes the National Housing Act.

April 1935
Roosevelt initiates the Resettlement Administration, designed to
deal with the severe problems of rural poverty.

August 1935
Congress passes the Wealth Tax Act, providing for higher taxes on
well-to-do Americans; the president signs the Social Security Act,
creating a national old-age pension system.

September 1935
Louisiana senator Huey Long, who had proposed a widely popular
wealth redistribution program ("Share the Wealth"), is assassinated
in Baton Rouge.

February 1936
The Supreme Court declares the Agricultural Adjustment Act
unconstitutional.

November 1936
Roosevelt is reelected, defeating his Republican opponent, Kansas
governor Alf Landon, by a crushing electoral margin of 523 to 8.

April 1937
The American economy finally reaches the level of output it had
maintained in 1929 before the beginning of the Depression.

May 1937
The Supreme Court upholds the constitutionality of the Social
Security Act.

August 1937
With recovery seemingly taking hold, the nation experiences a sud-
den recession, or economic downturn.

June 1938
Congress authorizes billions of dollars for new public works projects to fight the effects of the recent recession; Congress passes the
Fair Labor Standards Act, providing for a minimum wage of forty
cents an hour and a forty-hour work week.

September 1939
Raymond Moley, formerly one of Roosevelt's closest advisers, pub-
lishes his book *After Seven Years*, in which he severely criticizes the
president and the New Deal; war erupts in Europe as Germany, led
by Nazi dictator Adolf Hitler, invades Poland.

1941–1945
The United States fights in World War II against Germany, Italy,
and Japan; a virtual avalanche of American war production helps to
pull the nation the rest of the way out of the Depression.

April 1945
Franklin D. Roosevelt, architect of the New Deal and principal vic-
tor of World War II, dies at the age of sixty-three in the midst of his
fourth term as president; he is succeeded by Harry S. Truman.

STUDY QUESTIONS

Chapter 1

1. How does historian Charles Beard characterize the creed of "rugged individualism" in Viewpoint 1? What example does Franklin Roosevelt give of the Republicans violating this creed?

2. What role does Roosevelt believe the federal government should play in people's lives?

3. According to Herbert Hoover in Viewpoint 2, what are some of the traits of the "social system peculiarly our own"?

4. Why, according to Hoover and journalist Walter Lippmann in Viewpoint 2, is a buildup of the federal government potentially dangerous?

5. Contrast Hoover's view of self-reliance in Viewpoint 3 with Joseph Heffernan's warning about the destruction of self-respect in Viewpoint 4. After reading Viewpoints 3 and 4, explain why you think one is more convincing, given the circumstances of the early 1930s.

Chapter 2

1. In Viewpoint 1, what reasons does George Norris give for the redistribution of the nation's wealth?

2. List the major points of Senator Huey Long's plan for sharing the wealth.

3. In Viewpoint 2, how does Walter Lippmann support his statement that "a plan for production is incompatible with voluntary labor"?

4. Why, in Viewpoint 3, does Daniel Hastings fear that Social Security will harm American values?

5. According to Frances Perkins in Viewpoint 4, what are the main features of the Social Security Act?

6. Seek out and talk to three persons you know who are receiving Social Security benefits. Record their reactions to the views stated in Viewpoints 3 and 4.

7. According to Viewpoint 5, in what ways did black Americans benefit from the New Deal?

8. What, according to Edwin Hoyt, Harold Ickes, and Nate Shaw, are some of the obstacles blacks faced in the racist society of the 1930s? In your opinion, do blacks still face some of these obstacles? Give some examples of why they do or do not.

9. What are some of the ways cited in Viewpoint 6 in which the AAA discriminated against black Americans? How did the TVA discriminate?

Chapter 3

1. In Viewpoint 1, why, according to Hamilton Fish, were the inadequacies of the New Deal not well documented in the 1930s?

2. According to French journalist Amaury de Riencourt, what personal qualities did Roosevelt possess that allowed him to amass a great deal of power and still maintain widespread popular support?

3. List at least six important accomplishments of the New Deal, as presented in Viewpoint 2.

4. Contrast de Riencourt's image of Roosevelt as a benign dictator (Viewpoint 1) with Arthur Schlesinger's image of Roosevelt as a courageous national savior (Viewpoint 2). Based on what you have read about Roosevelt in this and other volumes, which of these images do you find more truthful? Why?

Special Project

A number of the viewpoints in this volume cite excerpts from famed journalist Studs Terkel's enlightening and entertaining book *Hard Times: An Oral History of the Great Depression* (see Major Works Consulted). Terkel interviewed over a hundred people from all walks of life who had lived through the social and economic upheaval of the 1930s, and their recorded impressions and personal stories constitute a unique and important commentary on the period.

In a similar manner, find at least five people who lived through the Depression. First, ask each of them to recount his or her personal situation during those times, including profession or school, living conditions, financial status, family relationships, and so on. Then interview each (a tape recorder is the best approach), asking questions formulated from the information in the viewpoints in this volume. For example, you might ask how the New Deal specifically affected the person and his or her family; whether he or she or a relative or friend was employed by the PWA, CCC, TVA, or other public works programs; whether the person remembers listening to Roosevelt's fireside chats and what he or she thought about the president and his New Dealers; and/or whether, thanks to the New Deal, his or her family was better or worse off by the early 1940s. When the interviews are completed, type and bind them, creating your own unique oral historical record of one of the most turbulent and dramatic periods in American history.

FOR FURTHER READING

Tricia Andryszewski, *The Dust Bowl: Disaster on the Plains.* Brookfield, CT: Millbrook Press, 1993. The gripping story of devastation of farms and massive displacement of farm families in the American heartland during the economic crisis of the 1930s. Well written and worthwhile.

Nancy M. Davies, *The Stock Market Crash of Nineteen Twenty-Nine.* Parsippany, NJ: Silver Burdett Press, 1994. This informative explanation of the workings of the stock market and analysis of the big crash that initiated the Great Depression provides excellent supplementary material for the present volume.

Karen McAuley, *Eleanor Roosevelt.* New York: Chelsea House, 1987. A commendable introduction to the unique personality and accomplishments of one of the most notable and charismatic of U.S. First Ladies, including her contributions to alleviating the Great Depression.

Joyce Moss and George Wilson, *Profiles in American History: Significant Events and the People Who Shaped Them.* Vol. 7: *The Great Depression to the Cuban Missile Crisis.* Detroit: Gale Research, 1995. Contains an informative overview of the Great Depression, concentrating on the large political and literary personalities involved, especially President Franklin D. Roosevelt, First Lady Eleanor Roosevelt, and John Steinbeck, author of *The Grapes of Wrath*, the famous novel about the effects of the crisis on farmers in the West and Midwest.

Don Nardo, *Franklin D. Roosevelt: U.S. President.* New York: Chelsea House, 1996. An easy-to-read, informative volume summarizing the life, struggles, and incredible accomplishments of one of the nation's greatest leaders, including descriptions of his election campaigns, his response to the Great Depression crisis, instigation of New Deal programs, steerage of the country through the crisis of World War II, and courageous response to the challenge of his daunting physical handicap.

——, *The U.S. Presidency.* San Diego: Lucent Books, 1995. This concise overview of the development of the office, its duties, and its impact on American history contains a section on Franklin D. Roosevelt and his avalanche of New Deal legislation.

Catherine O. Peare, *The Herbert Hoover Story.* New York: Thomas Y. Crowell, 1965. A concise overview of the life and times of the U.S. president on whose watch the stock exchange crashed and the Great Depression began. Geared for basic to intermediate readers.

Susan Renberger, *A Multicultural Portrait of the Great Depression.* Tarrytown, NY: Marshall Cavendish, 1995. An interesting and effective attempt to cover the Great Depression from the often neglected viewpoints of minority groups, many of whom suffered worse than average white Americans during the crisis.

Gail Stewart, *The New Deal.* Parsippany, NJ: Silver Burdett Press, 1993. This well-written synopsis of New Deal legislation, its controversies, and its effects is highly recommended.

MAJOR WORKS CONSULTED

Anthony J. Badger, *The New Deal: The Depression Years, 1933–1940*. New York: Farrar, Straus and Giroux, 1989. A very well written and informative general overview of the New Deal and how it affected the United States in the Depression years.

Kenneth S. Davis, *FDR: The New Deal Years, 1933–1937*. New York: Random House, 1986. Part of Davis's justly acclaimed series about various periods of Roosevelt's life, this volume provides a thorough, detailed account of his implementation of the New Deal. Highly recommended.

William Dudley, ed., *The Great Depression: Opposing Viewpoints*. San Diego: Greenhaven Press, 1994. A very useful collection of original articles, speeches, and other writings from and about the Depression era, including selections by Herbert Hoover and Franklin Roosevelt; historians Stuart Chase, Barton Bernstein, and William Leuchtenburg; economist Ray Vance; New Deal players Rex Tugwell, Henry Wallace, and Frances Perkins; Supreme Court justice Hugo Black; and many others.

Frank Freidel, *Franklin D. Roosevelt: A Rendezvous with Destiny*. Boston: Little, Brown, 1990. One of the three or four best available biographies of Roosevelt. Like Davis's, this is highly recommended.

Richard Hofstadter, ed., *Great Issues in American History: A Documentary Record, Volume II, 1864–1957*. New York: Vintage Books, 1960. A noted historian has here compiled a useful group of original documents from the last half of the nineteenth century and first half of the twentieth. Those concerning the Depression and New Deal include important campaign speeches by Hoover and Roosevelt, as well as the texts of Supreme Court decisions relating to the legality of New Deal programs.

Edwin P. Hoyt, *The Tempering Years*. New York: Charles Scribner's Sons, 1963. This interesting and informative book covers the decade of 1929 to 1939 by focusing in on the careers of various public figures who helped shape the events and opinions of that decade.

Harold L. Ickes, *The Secret Diary of Harold L. Ickes: The First Thousand Days, 1933–1936*. New York: Simon and Schuster,

1954. Part of the many-volume set of Ickes's personal journals about his life as a public servant in Washington, D.C. In his long and phenomenally detailed narrative (over six million words in all), Ickes, Roosevelt's secretary of the interior, captures many of the private moments and intimate personalities of just about every important public official of his day. This is fascinating and invaluable material for historians and devoted Roosevelt buffs; however, the average reader will need to have a good general synopsis of the period handy for frequent reference (those by Badger, Leuchtenburg, Schlesinger, and Watkins, cited above and below, are good bets).

Morton Keller, ed., *The New Deal: What Was It?* New York: Holt, Rinehart and Winston, 1963. A useful collection of essays by noted historians (including Daniel Boorstin, Richard Hofstadter, Basil Rauch, and Arthur Schlesinger) evaluating the effectiveness of Roosevelt's New Deal programs.

William E. Leuchtenburg, *Franklin D. Roosevelt and the New Deal, 1932–1940*. New York: Harper and Row, 1963. A noted historian's excellent and very carefully documented synopsis of the events and personalities of the New Deal period.

William E. Leuchtenburg, ed., *The New Deal: A Documentary History*. New York: Harper and Row, 1968. A hefty collection of articles, speeches, letters, and other original documents from the Depression era, including both pro and con opinions of Roosevelt and his policies.

Walter Lippmann, *The Good Society*. Boston: Little, Brown, 1937. This fascinating philosophical discussion of what a democratic people and their government should stand for was written at the height of and duly influenced by Roosevelt's implementation of the New Deal. Walter Lippmann (1889–1974) was a renowned Pulitzer Prize–winning journalist and social commentator (it is said that millions of Americans eagerly awaited reading his columns each morning so that they could "know what to think" about the issues of the day). I have had the honor of reading Mr. Lippmann's own copy, as his personal collection of books are collected in a special room at my local library (Centerville, Massachusetts).

Ted Morgan, *FDR: A Biography*. New York: Simon and Schuster, 1985. Another of the handful of best available and highly recommended Roosevelt biographies (see also those by Davis and Freidel above).

William S. Myers and Walter H. Newton, *The Hoover Administration: A Documented Narrative*. New York: Charles Scribner's Sons, 1936. This synopsis of Hoover's years in the White House reads like a diary, each succeeding date containing a concise summary of what happened that day (or series of days), often accompanied by fulsome extracts from the president's speeches and announcements. Will appeal mainly to scholars.

Basil Rauch, *A History of the New Deal, 1933–1938*. New York: Octagon Books, 1975. A noted historian here delivers an insightful summary of the major accomplishments of the New Deal; Rauch makes the point that many people hated the New Deal in the 1930s, but that such negative views became rare in the decades that followed. Today, he says, "it would be easier to raise a regiment to fight for the Confederacy than against the New Deal."

Theodore Rosengarten, *All God's Dangers: The Life of Nate Shaw*. New York: Knopf, 1974. This moving and fascinating book is a first-person narrative by a black cotton farmer born in Alabama in 1885. Through his own words, we see, often in vivid detail, how people, both black and white, lived in the rural South before the advent of the modern civil rights movement. Of special interest here are the sections covering the experiences of Shaw and other blacks during the Great Depression.

Samuel I. Rosenman, ed., *The Public Papers and Addresses of Franklin D. Roosevelt* (thirteen volumes). New York: Russell and Russell, 1969. This massive collection of FDR's speeches and public statements is an indispensable reference for any study of the Depression and the New Deal.

Elliot Roosevelt, ed., *FDR: His Personal Letters, 1928–1945* (two volumes). New York: Duell, Sloan and Pearce, 1950. Like the *Public Papers and Addresses* (above), this is basic and essential primary source material for studying the period of the 1930s.

Arthur M. Schlesinger Jr., *The Coming of the New Deal*. Boston: Houghton Mifflin, 1959. A very well written, researched, and documented overview of the first two years of Roosevelt's first term, including the "Hundred Days" and the country's initial response to the rapid implementation of the first New Deal programs.

John Steinbeck, *The Grapes of Wrath*. New York: Viking Press, 1939. Steinbeck's great novel examines in excruciating and moving detail the plight of a family of rural Americans caught in the "dust bowl" of destroyed farms and dreams that plagued the Midwest and West during the Depression years. Also look for the videotape of the excellent film version released in 1940, directed by John Ford and starring Henry Fonda.

Studs Terkel, *Hard Times: An Oral History of the Great Depression*. New York: Random House, 1970. Terkel (born 1912), a widely respected journalist, social commentator, and author, has gathered a fulsome and fascinating collection of remembrances of the Depression era by over 160 Americans from all walks of life.

T.H. Watkins, *The Great Depression: America in the 1930s*. Boston: Little, Brown and Company, 1993. This is one of the best recent overviews of the Depression and New Deal, featuring plenty of statistics, primary source commentary, and other supporting detail.

Howard Zinn, ed., *New Deal Thought*. Indianapolis: Bobbs-Merrill, 1966. A very useful collection of original articles, speeches, and other documents from the Depression era, edited by a noted historian.

ADDITIONAL WORKS CONSULTED

John Braeman et al., eds., *The New Deal: The National Level.* Columbus: Ohio State University Press, 1975.

Stuart Chase, *A New Deal.* New York: Macmillan, 1932.

Melvin Dubofsky and Stephen Burnwood, *Women and Minorities During the Great Depression.* New York: Garland, 1990.

James N. Gregory, *American Exodus: The Dust Bowl Migration and Okie Culture in California.* New York: Oxford University Press, 1989.

Richard Hofstadter et al., *The United States: The History of a Republic.* Englewood Cliffs, NJ: Prentice-Hall, 1957.

Herbert Hoover, *The Memoirs of Herbert Hoover: 1929–1941, The Great Depression.* New York: Macmillan, 1952.

Gerald W. Johnson, *Franklin D. Roosevelt: Portrait of a Great Man.* New York: William Morrow, 1967.

John B. Kirby, *Black Americans in the Roosevelt Era: Liberalism and Race.* Knoxville: University of Tennessee Press, 1980.

William K. Klingaman, *1929: The Year of the Great Crash.* New York: Harper and Row, 1989.

Joseph P. Lash, *Dealers and Dreamers: A New Look at the New Deal.* New York: Doubleday, 1988.

David Lawrence, *Beyond the New Deal.* New York: McGraw-Hill, 1934.

Robert McElvaine, *The Great Depression: America 1929–1941.* New York: Tomes Books, 1984.

Raymond Moley, *After Seven Years.* New York: Harper and Brothers, 1939.

Samuel Eliot Morison, *The Oxford History of the American People.* New York: Oxford University Press, 1965.

Richard H. Pells, *Radical Visions and American Dreams: Culture and Social Thought in the Depression Years.* New York: Harper and Row, 1973.

Frances Perkins, *The Roosevelt I Knew.* New York: Harper and Row, 1946.

Diane Ravitch, ed., *The American Reader: Words That Moved a Nation*. New York: HarperCollins, 1990.

Eleanor Roosevelt, *This I Remember*. New York: Harper and Brothers, 1949.

Edwin C. Rozwenc, ed., *The New Deal: Revolution or Evolution?* Boston: D.C. Heath, 1949.

Bonnie F. Schwartz, *The Civil Works Administration, 1933–1934: The Business of Emergency Employment in the New Deal*. Princeton, NJ: Princeton University Press, 1984.

Jordan A. Schwarz, *The New Dealers: Power Politics in the Age of Roosevelt*. New York: Knopf, 1993.

Gene Smith, *The Shattered Dream: Herbert Hoover and the Great Depression*. New York: Morrow, 1970.

Howard Zinn, *A People's History of the United States*. New York: HarperCollins, 1980.

INDEX

ABOUT THE AUTHOR

Historian and award-winning author Don Nardo has written many books for young adults about American history and government, including *The U.S. Presidency, The U.S. Congress, Democracy, The War of 1812, The Bill of Rights,* and *Franklin D. Roosevelt: U.S. President.* Mr. Nardo has also written several teleplays and screenplays, including work for Warner Brothers and ABC-Television. He lives with his wife, Christine, and dog, Bud, on Cape Cod, Massachusetts.